Second Edition

Program Manager
with Daily Lesson Plans

Ann D. Anderson
Nancy Wrobel
Leslie Caye Yeats

EMC/Paradigm Publishing, Saint Paul, Minnesota

ISBN 0-8219-2329-3

Published by EMC/Paradigm Publishing
875 Montreal Way
St. Paul, Minnesota 55102
800-328-1452
www.emcp.com
E-mail: educate@emcp.com

Printed in the United States of America
1 2 3 4 5 6 7 8 9 10 X X X 06 05 04 03 02 01

Table of Contents

Introduction

Every teacher knows how difficult lesson planning can be. Interruptions such as fire drills, pep assemblies and illness are just three examples of the many factors that affect instructional contact time and that require teachers to adjust their daily teaching syllabus. Furthermore, methodology, instructional time, philosophy and individual learner needs all vary greatly from one classroom to the next. Some schools offer traditional 45- to 55-minute classes, whereas other schools—sometimes within the same district—prefer a block scheduling system consisting of class periods that range from 75 to 110 minutes. For the above reasons, it is difficult to outline a detailed lesson plan that would suit all teachers without modification. However, this Program Manager with Daily Lesson Plans offers a sample framework suggesting how to use the textbook *Somos así LISTOS,* along with accompanying ancillaries. Two models are provided: one for a 50-minute class period meeting, and another for a 90-minute block. Adhering to the suggested lesson plans for either model would make it possible to cover all chapters of the textbook in one school year.

Somos así LISTOS is a flexible program and allows teachers to cover material in the textbook and ancillaries according to the degree of thoroughness suggested by student needs, time and personal teaching style or school resources. For example, some activities and the *Conexión cultural* notes may be omitted, depending upon the needs and time limitations set by individual circumstances. The reading section titled *A leer* is optional, thus offering you additional flexibility in matching content to the needs, interests and curriculum requirements of your own particular situation. Dialogs, other narrative material and many activities in *Somos así LISTOS* have been recorded and thus offer you additional choices about how to present or review the chapter content.

In general, try to vary your presentations by using as many different resources as possible in order to recombine similar material for your students' diverse learning styles. For example, the Audiocassette/Audio CD Program and the Teacher's Resource Kit offer listening comprehension practice; the Video Program allows students an opportunity to observe native speakers using Spanish in contexts that require skills your students are learning; Internet activities individualize and personalize instruction; overhead transparencies offer visual support of spoken Spanish and can serve to practice both rote material as well as to provide situational contexts for conversations; and the textbook, Workbook and Teacher's Resource Kit activities all offer additional writing practice. Many ancillaries are available to supplement the textbook. These program components provide an abundance of textbook-related activities to provide teaching formats that will enable you to customize your teaching to the many and varied learning styles and needs of your students.

Since every teacher has his or her own approach to the subject of homework, and due to the extensive variety offered by the *Somos así* support materials, specific homework assignments are not provided. However, suggestions for including activities from the accompanying ancillaries have been offered to give you an idea of the possible variations the teaching program offers.

REGULAR CLASS PERIOD (50 MINUTES)

Capítulo 1, lecciones 1 y 2

Day 1

Textbook	Support Materials
Chapter preview: Discuss chapter opener, pp. xxii and 1	AC/CD: *Conectados con el mundo* (Side A, track 1)
Conectados con el mundo, pp. 2-3	AC/CD: Activity 1 (Side A, track 2)
Activity 1, p. 3	Transparency 1
Algo más, p. 4	AC/CD: Activity 2 (Side A, track 3)
Para ti: ¿Inglés o español?, p. 4	Workbook Activity 1, p. 1
Activity 2, p. 4	Quiz/Written Activity 1, p. W1
Conexión cultural, p. 4	Workbook Activity 2, p. 2
Activity 3, p. 4	
Repaso rápido, p. 5	
Para ti: En los Apéndices, p. 5	
Activity 4, p. 5	

Notes

Day 2

Textbook	Support Materials
Warm-up: Review present tense verbs, including *estar, hacer, ir, ser, tener*, p. 5	Transparency 2
Activities 5-9, pp. 6-7	Quiz/Listening Activity 1, p. L1 (Side A, track 1)
Para ti: Más para hablar del tiempo, p. 7	Transparencies 3-4
Activities 10–11, p. 7	Workbook Activities 3-4, pp. 3-4
Repaso rápido, p. 8	AC/CD: Activity 12 (Side A, track 4)
Activity 12, p. 8	Quiz/Listening Activity 2, p. L2 (Side A, track 2)
Idioma, p. 9	Workbook Activities 5-6, pp. 5-6
Activity 13, p. 9	AC/CD: Activity 13 (Side A, track 5)
	Workbook Activity 7, p. 7
	Quiz/Written Activity 2, p. W2

Notes

Day 3

Textbook	Support Materials
Warm-up: Review the present progressive tense, *Repaso rápido*, p. 8	AC/CD: *La mejor compañera* (Side A, track 7)
Activity 14, p. 10	AC/CD: Activities 14-16 (Side A, tracks 6, 8 and 9)
La mejor compañera, p. 10	Workbook Activity 8, p. 8
Activities 15-16, pp. 10-11	Quiz/Listening Activity 3, p. L3 (Side A, track 3)
Para ti: Proverbios y dichos, p. 11	
Conexión cultural, p. 11	Workbook Activities 9-10, pp. 8-9
Activity 17, p. 12	Quiz/Written Activity 3, p. W3
Oportunidades, p. 12	Transparency 5
Repaso rápido, p. 12	
Activities 18-19, p. 13	
Para ti: ir a, p. 13	
Activity 20, p. 13	

Notes

Day 4

Textbook	Support Materials
Warm-up: Review stem-changing verbs, pp. 9 and 12	Workbook Activities 11-12, pp. 10-11
Idioma, p. 14	Quiz/Listening Activity 4, p. L4 (Side A, track 4)
Activities 21-22, p. 15	Workbook Activities 13-14, p. 12
Algo más, p. 15	Quiz/Written Activity 4, p. W4
Activities 23-25, p. 16	Oral Proficiency Evaluation Manual, Activities 1-3, pp. 1-3
Autoevaluación, p. 17	Select an activity from *Capítulo 1* to include in the *Somos así* Portfolio Assessment. Suggestion: Activity A, p. 18, Appendices B and F
¡La práctica hace al maestro!, Activities A-B, p. 18	
Review for the test on *Lección 1*	

Notes

Day 5

Textbook	Support Materials
Test on *Lección 1*	Student Test Booklet, Activities 1-14, pp. 1-8
	Test Booklet Teacher's Edition, pp. 1-3
	Audiocassette/Audio CD listening comprehension test (Side A, tracks 1-5)
	Oral Proficiency Evaluation Manual, Activities 1-3, pp. 1-3
	Select an Activity from *Capítulo 1* to include in the *Somos así* Portfolio Assessment. Suggestion: Activity A, p. 18, Appendices B and F

Notes

Day 6

Textbook	Support Materials
Warm-up: Review *Vocabulario*, p. 19	AC/CD: *Escuela virtual* (Side B, track 10)
Review the test on *Lección 1*	Transparencies 6-7
¿Qué hiciste el pasado mes de junio?, p. 20	AC/CD: Activities 1-2 (Side B, tracks 11-12)
Activities 1-2, p. 21	Workbook Activity 1, p. 13
Para ti: Acabar de, p. 21	Quiz/Listening Activity 1, p. L5 (Side A, track 5)
Conexión cultural, p. 21	
Activity 3, p. 22	Workbook Activities 2-5, pp. 14-17
Oportunidades, p. 22	Quiz/Written Activity 1, W5
Repaso rápido, pp. 22-23	AC/CD: Activity 4 (Side B, track 13)
Activities, 4-5, p. 23	

Notes

Day 7

Textbook	Support Materials
Warm-up: Review irregular preterite verbs, pp. 22-23	AC/CD: *Después de clases* (Side B, tracks 14-15)
Activities 6-8, pp. 24-25	Transparencies 8-9
Después de clases, p. 25	AC/CD: Activities 9-10 (Side B, tracks 16-17)
Activities 9-10, p. 26	Quiz/Listening Activity 2, p. L6 (Side A, track 6)
Para ti: Más quehaceres en la casa, p. 26	
Algo más, p. 26	Workbook Activities 6-8, pp. 18-20
Repaso rápido, p. 27	Quiz/Written Activity 2, p. W6
Activity 11, p. 27	

Notes

Day 8

Textbook	Support Materials
Warm-up: Review direct and indirect object pronouns, pp. 26-27	Transparency 10
Activities 12-15, pp. 28-29	Workbook Activity 9, p. 21
Idioma, p. 30	Quiz/Written Activity 3, p. W7
Activities 16-19, pp. 30-31	AC/CD: Activity 19 (Side B, track 18)
Algo más, p. 32	Quiz/Listening Activity 3, p. L7 (Side A, track 7)
Activities 20-22, pp. 32-33	Workbook Activities 10-11, pp. 22-23
	Quiz/Written Activity 4, p. W8

Notes

Day 9

Textbook	Support Materials
Warm-up: Review double object pronoun use, p. 30 *Autoevaluación*, p. 33 *¡La práctica hace al maestro!*, Activities A-B, p. 34 *A leer*, Activities A-B, pp. 36-37 *A escribir*, p. 38 Review for the test on *Lección 2*	Workbook Activity 12, p. 24 AC/CD: *En la Internet* (Side B, track 19) AC/CD: Activities A-B (Side B, tracks 20-21) Video Program, Episode 1 Oral Proficiency Evaluation Manual, Activities 1-3, pp. 4-6 Select an activity from *Capítulo 1* to include in the *Somos así* Portfolio Assessment. Suggestion: Checklist appropriate items on appendices F, G, H, I and J, as needed.

Notes

Day 10

Textbook	Support Materials
Test on *Lección 2*	Student Test Booklet, Activities 1-16, pp. 9-16 Test Booklet Teacher's Edition, pp. 3-6 Audiocassette/Audio CD listening comprehension test (Side A, tracks 6-11) Oral Proficiency Evaluation Manual, Activities 1-3, pp. 4-6 Select an activity from *Capítulo 1* to include in the *Somos así* Portfolio Assessment. Suggestion: Checklist appropriate items on appendices F, G, H, I and J, as needed.

Notes

Capítulo 2, lecciones 3 y 4

Day 1

Textbook	Support Materials
Warm-up: *Repaso*, p. 39	AC/CD: *Somos muy diferentes.* (Side A, tracks 1-2)
Review the test on *Lección 2*	Workbook Activity 1, p. 25
Chapter preview: Discuss chapter opener, pp. 40-41	AC/CD Activities 1-2 (Side A, tracks 3-4)
Somos muy diferentes, p. 42	Quiz/Written Activity 1, p. W9
Activity 1, p. 43	
Para ti: Hablando del pelo, p. 43	
Activities 2-3, p. 43	

Notes

Day 2

Textbook	Support Materials
Warm-up: Review vocabulary from *Somos muy diferentes*, p. 42	AC/CD: *Lugares en los Estados Unidos con nombres en español* (Side A, track 5)
Conexión cultural, p. 44	Transparency 11
Activity 4, p. 44	Workbook Activity 2, p. 26
Oportunidades, p. 45	Quiz/Written Activity 2, p. W10
Activity 5, p. 45	

Notes

Day 3

Textbook	Support Materials
Warm-up: Review *Oportunidades*, p. 45 *Idioma*, pp. 45-46 Activity 6, p. 46	Quiz/Listening Activity 1, p. L9 (Side A, track 8) Workbook Activities 3-4, pp. 27-28 Quiz/Listening Activity 2, p. L9 (Side A, track 9)

Notes

Day 4

Textbook	Support Materials
Warm-up: Review *los verbos reflexivos*, p. 45 *Algo más*, p. 46 Activities 7-11, pp. 47-48	Transparency 12 Workbook Activity 5, p. 29 Quiz/Written Activity 3, p. W11 AC/CD: Activities 9-11 (Side A, tracks 6-8)

Notes

Day 5

Textbook	Support Materials
Warm-up: Review reflexive vs. nonreflexive verb forms, p. 46 *Estrategia,* p. 49 *Para ti: Proverbios y dichos,* p. 49 Activities 12-13, pp. 49-50 *Algo más,* p. 50 Activities 14-17, pp. 50-51	Quiz/Written Activity 4, p. W12

Notes

Day 6

Textbook	Support Materials
Warm-up: Review *el artículo definido con verbos reflexivos,* p. 50 *Algo más,* p. 52 Activities 18-19, pp. 52-53 *Idioma,* p. 53 Activity 20, p. 53	Quiz/Listening Activity 3, p. L10 (Side A, track 10) Workbook Activity 6, p. 29 Quiz/Written Activity 5, p. W13 AC/CD: Activity 20 (Side A, track 9) Quiz/Listening Activity 4, p. L10 (Side A, track 11) Workbook Activities 7-8, p. 30

Notes

Day 7

Textbook	Support Materials
Warm-up: Review *el pretérito de los verbos reflexivos*, p. 52	Quiz/Listening Activity 5, p. L11 (Side A, track 12)
Conexión cultural, p. 54	Quiz/Written Activity 6, p. W14
Activities 21-22, p. 55	AC/CD: *Una toalla, por favor* (Side A, track 10)
Una toalla, por favor, p. 55	Quiz/Listening Activity 6, p. L12
	Transparencies 13-14
	Workbook Activities 9-10, pp. 31-32

Notes

Day 8

Textbook	Support Materials
Warm-up: Review asking and answering personal questions using the preterite tense	AC/CD: Activity 24 (Side A, track 11)
Para ti: Otras palabras y expresiones, p. 56	Quiz/Listening Activity 7, p. L12 (Side A, track 14)
Activities 23-25, p. 56	Workbook Activity 11, p. 33
Repaso rápido, p. 57	Quiz/Written Activity 7, p. W14
Idioma, p. *57*	
Activities 26-28, pp. 58-59	

Notes

Day 9

Textbook

Warm-up: Review *los adjetivos y pronombres demostrativos*, p. 57
¡La práctica hace al maestro!, Activities A-B, p. 60
Practice *Vocabulario*, p. 61
Autoevaluación, p. 59
Review for the test on *Lección 3*

Support Materials

Workbook Activity 12, p. 34
Oral Proficiency Evaluation Manual, Activities 1-3, pp. 7-9
Select an activity from *Capítulo 2* to include in the *Somos así* Portfolio Assessment. Suggestion: Activity 18, p. 52, Appendices B and F

Notes

Day 10

Textbook

Test on *Lección 3*

Support Materials

Student Test Booklet, Activities 1-13, pp. 17-24
Test Booklet Teacher's Edition, pp. 6-9
Audiocassette/Audio CD listening comprehension test (Side A, tracks 12-15)
Oral Proficiency Evaluation Manual, Activities 1-3, pp. 7-9
Select an activity from *Capítulo 2* to include in the *Somos así* Portfolio Assessment. Suggestion: Activity 18, p. 52, Appendices B and F

Notes

Day 11

Textbook	Support Materials
Warm-up: Review reflexive verbs	AC/CD: *No me siento bien* (Side B, track 13)
Review the test on *Lección 3*	
No me siento bien, p. 62	AC/CD: Activity 1 (Side B, track 14)
Para ti: La palabra pescar, p. 62	Workbook Activity 1, p. 35
Activities 1-2, pp. 62-63	AC/CD: Activity 2 (Side B, track 15)
Conexión cultural, p. 63	AC/CD: *Aquí se habla español* (Side B, track 16)
	Workbook Activity 2, p. 36
	Quiz/Written Activity 1, p. W15

Notes

Day 12

Textbook	Support Materials
Warm-up: Review dialog on p. 62	Quiz/Written Activity 2, p. W16
Activity 3, p. 64	AC/CD: *El cuerpo* (Side B, track 17)
Oportunidades, p. 64	Quiz/Listening Activity 1, p. L13 (Side A, track 15)
Activity 4, p. 64	
El cuerpo, p. 65	Transparencies 15-16
Activity 5, p. 65	Workbook Activities 3-4, pp. 36-37
Para ti: Más palabras del cuerpo, p. 65	

Notes

Day 13

Textbook	Support Materials
Warm-up: Review *El cuerpo*, p. 65	AC/CD: Activity 8 (Side B, track 18)
Activities 6-8, p. 66	Quiz/Listening Activity 2, p. L14 (Side A, track 16)
Algo más, p. 67	Workbook Activity 5, p. 38
Activities 9-10, p. 67	Quiz/Written Activity 3, p. W17

Notes

Day 14

Textbook	Support Materials
Warm-up: Review *¿Qué oyes en el consultorio del médico?*, p. 67	AC/CD: Activity 11 (Side B, track 19)
	Workbook Activity 6, p. 39
Activity 11, p. 68	Quiz/Written Activity 4, p. W18
Idioma, p. 68	AC/CD: Activity 14 (Side B, track 20)
Activities 12-14, pp. 68-69	Workbook Activity 7, p. 40
Algo más, p. 69	Quiz/Written Activity 5, p. W18

Notes

Day 15

Textbook	Support Materials
Warm-up: Review *Más sobre los verbos reflexivos*, p. 69 Activities 15-17, pp. 70-71 *En el médico*, p. 71 Activity 18, p. 72	AC/CD: *En el médico* (Side B, tracks 21-22) Quiz/Listening Activity 3, p. L14 (Side A, track 17) AC/CD: Activity 18 (Side B, track 23)

Notes

Day 16

Textbook	Support Materials
Warm-up: Review the dialog *En el médico*, p. 71 *Para ti: ¿Doctor?*, p. 72 Activities 19-20, p. 72 *Algo más*, p. 73 Activity 21, p. 73	AC/CD: Activity 19 (Side B, track 24) Quiz/Listening Activity 4, p. L15 (Side A, track 18) Workbook Activities 8-9, pp. 40-42

Notes

Day 17

Textbook	Support Materials
Warm-up: Review *Verbos similares*, p. 73	Quizzes/Listening Activities 5-6, pp. L15-L16 (Side A, tracks 19-20)
Activity 22, p. 74	Workbook Activity 10, p. 43
Repaso rápido, p. 74	Quiz/Written Activity 6, p. W19
Idioma, p. 74	AC/CD: Activities 23-24 (Side B, tracks 25-26)
Activities 23-25, p. 75	
Autoevaluación, p. 75	

Notes

Day 18

Textbook	Support Materials
Warm-up: Review *Las preposiciones* and *Los verbos después de las preposiciones*, p. 74	Workbook Activity 11, p. 44
¡*La práctica hace al maestro!*, Activities A-B, p. 76	Video Program, Episode 2
Review *Vocabulario*, p. 77	Oral Proficiency Evaluation Manual, Activities, Activities 1-3, pp. 10-12
	Select an activity from *Capítulo 2* to include in the *Somos así* Portfolio Assessment. Suggestion: Checklist appropriate items on appendices F, G, H, I and J, as needed.

Notes

Day 19

Textbook	Support Materials
Warm-up: Review reflexive verbs *A leer,* Activities A-B, pp. 78-79 *A escribir,* p. 80 Review for the test on *Lección 4*	AC/CD: *La vida de una atleta profesional* (Side B, track 27) AC/CD: Activities A-B (Side B, tracks 28-29) Quiz/Listening Activity 7, p. L16 (Side A, track 21) Quiz/Written Activity 7, p. W20

Notes

Day 20

Textbook	Support Materials
Test on *Lección 4*	Student Test Booklet, Activities 1-12, pp. 25-32 Test Booklet Teacher's Edition, pp. 9-11 Audiocassette/Audio CD listening comprehension test (Side A, tracks 16-19) Oral Proficiency Evaluation Manual, Activities, Activities 1-3, pp. 10-12 Select an activity from *Capítulo 2* to include in the *Somos así* Portfolio Assessment. Suggestion: Checklist appropriate items on appendices F, G, H, I and J, as needed.

Notes

Capítulo 3, lecciones 5 y 6

Day 1

Textbook	Support Materials
Warm-up: Review everyday activities, commands (used in a doctor's office), foods	AC/CD: *En la ciudad* (Side A, tracks 1-2)
Review the test on *Lección 4*	Quiz/Listening Activity 1, p. L17 (Side B, track 22)
Chapter preview: Discuss chapter opener, pp. 82-83	Transparencies 17-18
En la ciudad, p. 84	Workbook Activity 1, p. 45
Activities 1-2, p. 85	AC/CD: Activities 1-2 (Side A, tracks 3-4)
Conexión cultural, p. 86	Quiz/Written Activity 1, pp. W21-W22
Activity 3, p. 87	AC/CD: *México* (Side A, track 5)
Estrategia, p. 87	Quiz/Listening Activity 2, p. L18 (Side B, track 23)
Algo más, p. 87	Workbook Activity 2, p. 46
Para ti: Más tiendas en la ciudad, p. 87	AC/CD: Activity 3 (Side A, track 6)
Activity 4, p. 88	Quiz/Listening Activity 3, p. L18 (Side B, track 24)
	Transparency 19
	Workbook Activity 3, p. 46
	Quiz/Written Activity 2, p. W23
	AC/CD: Activity 4 (Side A, track 7)

Notes

Day 2

Textbook	Support Materials
Warm-up: Review *Estrategia,* p. 87	AC/CD: Activities 5-6 (Side A, tracks 8-9)
Activities 5-6, pp. 88-89	Quiz/Listening Activity 4, p. L19 (Side B, track 25)
Idioma, p. 89	Workbook Activities 4-6, pp. 47-49
Para ti: Proverbios y dichos, p. 90	Quizzes/Written Activities 3-4, pp. W25-W26
Activities 7-8, p. 90	

Notes

Day 3 | **Textbook** | **Support Materials**

Warm-up: Review dialog, p. 84 and
    affirmative informal commands, p. 89
Activities 9-12, pp. 91-92

AC/CD: *En la ciudad* (Side A, tracks 1-2)

Notes

Day 4 | **Textbook** | **Support Materials**

Warm-up: Review, talk with students about
    Mexican-American foods they have eaten
¿Qué le gustaría ordenar?, p. 93
Activity 13, p. 93
Para ti: *Más palabras,* p. 93
Conexión cultural, pp. 94-95
Activities 14-15, p. 96
Oportunidades, p. 96

AC/CD: *¿Qué le gustaría ordenar?* (Side B,
    track 10)
AC/CD: Activity 13 (Side B, track 11)
Workbook Activity 7, p. 50
Quiz/Written Activity 5, pp. W26-W27
AC/CD: Activity 14 (Side B, track 12)

Notes

Day 5

Textbook	Support Materials
Warm-up: Review *¿Qué le gustaría ordenar?*, p. 93	AC/CD: *¿Qué le gustaría ordenar?* (Side B, track 10)
Idioma, p. 97	Quizzes/Listening Activities 5-6, pp. L19-L20 (Side B, tracks 26-27)
Activities 16-19, pp. 98-99	Workbook Activities 8-9, p. 51
	Quiz/Written 6, p. W27
	AC/CD: Activity 19 (Side B, track 13)

Notes

Day 6

Textbook	Support Materials
Warm-up: Review affirmative formal commands, p. 97	AC/CD: Activities 20-21 (Side B, tracks 14-15)
Algo más, p. 100	Workbook Activity 10, p. 52
Activities 20-22, pp. 100-101	

Notes

Day 7	**Textbook**	**Support Materials**
	Warm-up: Review affirmative and formal commands, pp. 89 and 97	Quiz/Listening Activity 7, p. L20 (Side B, track 28)
	Idioma, p. 101	Workbook Activity 11, p. 53
	Activities 23-25, pp. 102-103	Quiz/Written Activity 7, p. W28
		AC/CD: Activity 23 (Side B, track 16)

Notes

Day 8	**Textbook**	**Support Materials**
	Warm-up: Review affirmative commands, pp. 89, 97 and 101	Workbook Activity 12, p. 54
	Autoevaluación, p. 103	
	¡La práctica hace al maestro!, Activity A, p. 104	

Notes

Day 9

Textbook	Support Materials
Warm-up: Review for the test on *Lección 5* ¡*La práctica hace al maestro!*, Activity B, p. 104	Oral Proficiency Evaluation Manual, Activities 1-3, pp. 13-15 Select an activity from *Capítulo 3* to include in the *Somos así* Portfolio Assessment. Suggestion: Activity A, p. 104, Appendices B and F

Notes

Day 10

Textbook	Support Materials
Test on *Lección 5*	Student Test Booklet, Activities 1-13, pp. 33-40 Test Booklet Teacher's Edition, pp. 11-14 Audiocassette/Audio CD listening comprehension test (Side B, tracks 20-23) Oral Proficiency Evaluation Manual, Activities 1-3, pp. 13-15 Select an activity from *Capítulo 3* to include in the *Somos así* Portfolio Assessment. Suggestion: Activity A, p. 104, Appendices B and F

Notes

Day 11

Textbook	Support Materials
Warm-up: Review places in the city, affirmative commands	AC/CD: *En el barrio Las Lomas* (Side A, tracks 1-2)
Review the test on *Lección 5*	AC/CD: Activity 1 (Side A, track 3)
En el barrio Las Lomas, p. 106	Quiz/Listening Activity 1, p. L21 (Side B, track29)
Activity 1, p. 106	Workbook Activity 1, p. 55
Algo más, p. 107	AC/CD: Activity 2 (Side A, track 4)
Activity 2, p. 107	Quiz/Listening Activity 2, p. L22 (Side B, track 30)
Oportunidades, p. 107	Workbook Activity 2, p. 56

Notes

Day 12

Textbook	Support Materials
Warm-up: Review *En el barrio Las Lomas,* p. 106	AC/CD: *México hoy* (Side A. track 5)
Conexión cultural, p. 108	Quiz/Listening Activity 3, p. L22 (Side B, track 31)
Activity 3, p. 109	Workbook Activities 3-5, pp. 57-58
Idioma, p. 110	Quiz/Written Activity 1, p. W29
Activities 4-6, p. 111	AC/CD: Activities 5-6 (Side A, tracks 6-7)

Notes

Day 13 | **Textbook** | **Support Materials**

Warm-up: Review *conocer* and *saber,* p. 110
Activities 7-9, p. 112
Algo más, p. 113
Activities 10-11, pp. 113-114

AC/CD: Activity 9 (Side A, track 8)
Workbook Activity 6, p. 59
Quiz/Written Activity 2, p. W30
AC/CD: Activity 11 (Side A, track 9)

Notes

Day 14 | **Textbook** | **Support Materials**

Warm-up: Review the formation of
    affirmative commands
En casa de Pablo, p. 115
Activities 12-13, p. 115
Idioma, p. 116
Activities 14-16, pp. 116-117

AC/CD: *En casa de Pablo* (Side B, track 10)
AC/CD: Activities 12-13 (Side B, tracks
    11-12)
Quiz/Listening Activity 4, p. L 23 (Side B,
    track 32)
Workbook Activities 7-8, pp. 59-60
Quizzes/Written Activities 3-4,
    pp. W31-W32
AC/CD: Activities 15-16 (Side B, tracks
    13-14)

Notes

Day 15

Textbook	Support Materials
Warm-up: Review negative commands, p. 116	Quiz/Listening Activity 5, p. L23 (Side B, track 33)
Activities 17-20, pp. 118-119	Workbook Activity 9, p. 61
Algo más, p. 119	Quiz/Written Activity 5, p. W33
Activities 21-22, p. 120	AC/CD: Activity 21 (Side B, track 15)

Notes

Day 16

Textbook	Support Materials
Warm-up: Review negative commands, pp. 116 and 119	AC/CD: *¡Qué coches!* (Side B, tracks 16-17)
Activities 23-24, p. 121	AC/CD: Activity 25 (Side B, track 18)
¡Qué coches!, p. 122	Transparencies 20-21
Para ti: Más palabras para el coche, p. 122	Workbook Activities 10-11, pp.62-63
Activities 25-27, pp. 122-123	Quiz/Written Activity 6, p. W34-W35
	AC/CD: Activity 27 (Side B, track 19)

Notes

Day 17

Textbook	Support Materials
Warm-up: Review vocabulary associated with getting around in a city *Las señales de tráfico,* p. 124 Activity 28, p. 124 *¡La práctica hace al maestro!,* Activities A-B, p. 126	AC/CD: *Las señales de tráfico* (Side B, track 20) Quiz/Listening Activity 6, p. L 24 (Side B, track 34) Transparencies 22-25 Workbook Activities 12, p. 64

Notes

Day 18

Textbook	Support Materials
Warm-up: Review discussion about Mexico *¡Conozca México!,* p. 128 *A leer,* Activities A-B, p. 128-129	AC/CD: *¡Conozca México!* (Side B, track 21) Quiz/Written Activity 7, p. W36 AC/CD: Activities A-B (Side B, tracks 22-23) Video Program, Episode 3

Notes

Day 19

Textbook	Support Materials
Warm-up: Review what students have learned about Mexico *Autoevaluación,* p. 125 Review for the test on *Lección 6* *A escribir,* p. 130	Oral Proficiency Evaluation Manual, Activities 1-3, pp. 16-18 Select an activity from *Capítulo 3* to include in the *Somos así* Portfolio Assessment. Suggestion: Checklist items on appendices C, D, E, F, G, H, I and J, as needed.

Notes

Day 20

Textbook	Support Materials
Test on *Lección 6*	Student Test Booklet, Activities 1-15, pp. 41-48 Test Booklet Teacher's Edition, pp. 14-17 Audiocassette/Audio CD listening comprehension test (Side B, tracks 24-28) Oral Proficiency Evaluation Manual, Activities 1-3, pp. 16-18 Select an activity from *Capítulo 3* to include in the *Somos así* Portfolio Assessment. Suggestion: Checklist items on appendices C, D, E, F, G, H, I and J, as needed.

Notes

Capítulo 4, lecciones 7 y 8

Day 1

Textbook	Support Materials
Warm-up: Review *Partes del coche*, p. 127 Review the test on *Lección 6* Chapter preview: Discuss chapter opener, pp. 132-133 *Un día en el parque de atracciones*, pp. 134-135 Activities 1-3, p. 135	AC/CD: *Un día en el parque de atracciones* (Side A, tracks 1-2) Quiz/Listening Activity 1, p. L25 (Side A, track 1) Transparencies 26-27 Workbook Activity 1, p. 65 AC/CD: Activities 1-2 (Side A, tracks 3-4)

Notes

Day 2

Textbook	Support Materials
Warm-up: Review the vocabulary from *Un día en el parque de atracciones*, p. 134 *Conexión cultural*, p. 136 Activity 4, p. 137 *Oportunidades*, p. 137 *Idioma*, pp. 137-138	AC/CD: *El Salvador* (Side A, track 5) Quiz/Listening Activity 2, p. L25 (Side A, track 2) Workbook Activity 2, p. 66 Quiz/Listening Activity 3, p. L26 (Side A, track 3) Workbook Activities 3-4, pp. 67-68 Quiz/Written Activity 1, p. W37

Notes

Day 3	Textbook	Support Materials
	Warm-up: Review *el imperfecto de los verbos regulares*, pp. 137-138 Activities 5-8, pp. 139-140 *Algo más*, p. 140 Activities 9-10, p. 141	AC/CD: Activities 5-6 (Side A, tracks 6-7) Workbook Activities 5-6, p. 69 Quiz/Written Activity 2, p. W38 AC/CD: Activity 9 (Side A, track 8)

Notes

Day 4	Textbook	Support Materials
	Warm-up: Review *Los usos del imperfecto*, p. 140 Activities 11-12, p. 142 *Una visita al jardín zoológico*, p. 143 Activity 13, p. 144	AC/CD: Activity 11 (Side A, track 9) AC/CD: *Una visita al jardín zoológico* (Side B, tracks 10-11) Quiz/Listening Activity 4, p. L27 (Side A, track 4) Transparencies 28-29 Workbook Activities 7-8, p. 70 Quiz/Written Activity 3, p. W39 AC/CD: Activity 13 (Side B, track 12)

Notes

Day 5 | **Textbook** | **Support Materials**

Warm-up: Review the dialog *Una visita al jardín zoológico,* p. 143
Algo más, p. 144
Activity 14, p. 144
Algo más, p. 145
Para ti: Más animales, p. 145
Activities 15-16, pp. 145-146

AC/CD: Activity 14 (Side B, track 13)
Quiz/Written Activity 4, p. W40

Notes

Day 6 | **Textbook** | **Support Materials**

Warm-up: Review animal vocabulary
Idioma, p. 146
Algo más, p. 146
Activities 17-18, p. 147
Para ti: Los monos, p. 147
Activity 19, p. 148

Quizzes/Listening Activities 5-6, pp. L127-L128 (Side A, tracks 5-6)
Workbook Activities 9-11, pp. 71-72
Quizzes/Written Activities 5-6, pp. W40-W41
AC/CD: Activity 18 (Side B, track 14)
Transparency 30

Notes

Day 7	Textbook	Support Materials
	Warm-up: Review *Más sobre los usos del imperfecto*, p. 146	AC/CD: Activity 20 and 22 (Side B, tracks 15-16)
	Activities 20-21, p. 149	Workbook Activity 12, p. 73
	Estrategia, p. 150	Quiz/Listening Activity 7, p. L28 (Side A, track 7)
	Activities 22-23, pp. 150-151	
	Algo más, p. 151	Workbook Activity 13, pp. 74-75
	Activity 24, p. 152	Quiz/Written Activity 7, p. W42

Notes

Day 8	Textbook	Support Materials
	Warm-up: Review *Las nacionalidades*, p. 151	AC/CD: Activity 28 (Side B, track 17)
	Activities 25-26, pp. 152-153	Oral Proficiency Evaluation Manual, Activities 1-3, pp. 19-21
	Repaso rápido, p. 153	
	Activities 27-28, pp. 154-155	

Notes

Day 9	**Textbook**	**Support Materials**

Warm up: Review the uses of *ser* vs. *estar*, p. 153

Autoevaluación, p. 155

¡La práctica hace al maestro!, Activities A-B, p. 156

Review *Vocabulario,* p. 157

Review for the test on *Lección 7*

Workbook Activity 14, p. 76

Select an activity from *Capítulo 4* to include in the *Somos así* Portfolio Assessment. Suggestion: Activity 27, p. 154, Appendices B and F

Notes

Day 10	**Textbook**	**Support Materials**

Test on *Lección 7*

Student Test Booklet, Activities 1-13, pp. 49-56

Test Booklet Teacher's Edition, pp. 17-19

Audiocassette/Audio CD listening comprehension test (Side A, tracks 1-4)

Oral Proficiency Evaluation Manual, Activities 1-3, pp. 19-21

Select an activity from *Capítulo 4* to include in the *Somos así* Portfolio Assessment. Suggestion: Activity 27, p. 154, Appendices B and F

Notes

Day 11	**Textbook**	**Support Materials**
	Warm-up: Review nationalities and animal vocabulary Review the test on *Lección 7* *El Gran Circo de las Estrellas,* p. 158 Activities 1-3, p. 159	AC/CD: *El Gran Circo de las Estrellas* (Side A, tracks 1-2) Quiz/Listening Activity 1, p. L 29 (Side A, track 8) Transparencies 31-32 Workbook Activity 1, p. 77 AC/CD: Activities 1-2 (Side A, tracks 3-4)

Notes

Day 12	**Textbook**	**Support Materials**
	Warm-up: Review the dialog *El Gran Circo de las Estrellas,* p. 158 *Conexión cultural,* p. 160 Activity 4, p. 161 *Idioma,* p. 161 Activities 5-7, p. 162	AC/CD: *Honduras* (Side A, track 5) Quiz/Listening Activity 2, p. L30 (Side A, track 9) Workbook Activities 2-4, pp. 78-79 Quiz/Written Activity 1, p. W43

Notes

Day 13 | **Textbook** | **Support Materials**

Warm-up: Review *Idioma*, p. 161
Repaso rápido, p. 163
Activities 8-9, p. 164
Idioma, pp. 165-166
Activity 10, p. 166

Quiz/Written Activity 2, p. W44
AC/CD: Activity 9 (Side A, track 6)
Quiz/Listening Activity 3, p. L30 (Side A, track 10)
Workbook Activities 5-6, pp. 80-81
Quiz/Written Activity 3, p. W45

Notes

Day 14 | **Textbook** | **Support Materials**

Warm-up: Review *Los adjetivos y su posición*, p. 165
Activities 11-12, p. 167
Para ti: Los adjetivos como sustantivos, p. 167
Activity 13, p. 168
¿Qué pasó en la finca?, pp. 168-169
Activities 14-17, p. 169

Transparency 33
AC/CD: *¿Qué pasó en la finca?* (Side B, tracks 7-8)
Quiz/Listening Activity 4, p. L31 (Side A, track 11)
Transparencies 34-35
Workbook Activity 7, p. 82
Quiz/Written Activity 4, p. W46
AC/CD: Activities 14, 15 and 17 (Side B, tracks 9-11)

Notes

Day 15

Textbook	Support Materials
Warm-up: Review the dialog/vocabulary *¿Qué pasó en la finca?*, pp. 168-169	AC/CD: *Lo que los animales dicen* (Side B, track 12)
Activity 18, p. 170	Quiz/Listening Activity 5, p. L31 (Side A, track 12)
Lo que los animales dicen, p. 170	Workbook Activities 8-9, p. 83
Algo más, p. 170	Quiz/Written Activity 5, p. W46
Activity 19, p. 171	
Para ti: Proverbios y dichos, p. 171	
Activity 20, p. 171	
Idioma, p. 172	

Notes

Day 16

Textbook	Support Materials
Warm-up: Review *Los adjetivos posesivos: formas largas*, p. 172	AC/CD: Activity 21 (Side B, track 13)
Algo más, p. 170	Workbook Activity 10, p. 84
Activities 21-24, pp. 173-174	Quiz/Written Activity 6, p. W47
Algo más, p. 174	AC/CD: Activity 26 (Side B, track 14)
Activities 25-26, pp. 174-175	

Notes

Textbook	Support Materials
Warm-up: Review *Los adjetivos y pronombres posesivos*, pp. 172 and 174 *Algo más*, p. 175 Activity 27, p. 176 *Algo más*, p. 176 Activity 28, pp. 176-177 *Autoevaluación*, p. 177	Workbook Activity 11, p. 85 AC/CD: Activity 27 (Side B, track 15) Quiz/Listening Activity 6, p. L32 (Side A, track 13) Workbook Activity 12, p. 85

Notes

Textbook	Support Materials
Warm-up: Review **Lo** *con adjetivos/adverbios*, p. 175 *¡La práctica hace al maestro!*, Activities A-B, p. 178 Review *Vocabulario*, p. 179 *A leer*, Activities A-B, pp. 180-181	Workbook Activity 13, p. 86 AC/CD: *¡El Gran Circo de los Hermanos Suárez!* (Side B, track 16) AC/CD: Activities A-B (Side B, tracks 17-18) Quiz/Listening Activity 7, p. L33 (Side A, track 14) Quiz/Written Activity 7, p. W48

Notes

Day 19

Textbook	Support Materials
Warm-up: Review circus and farm vocabulary, p. 179 *A escribir,* p. 182 Review for the test on *Lección* 8	Video Program, Episode 4 Oral Proficiency Evaluation Manual, Activities 1-3, pp. 22-24 Select an activity from *Capítulo 4* to include in the *Somos así* Portfolio Assessment. Suggestion: Checklist appropriate items on appendices F, G, H, I and J, as needed.

Notes

Day 20

Textbook	Support Materials
Test on *Lección* 8	Student Test Booklet, Activities 1-12, pp. 57-64 Test Booklet Teacher's Edition, pp. 20-22 Audiocassette/Audio CD listening comprehension test (Side A, tracks 5-8) Oral Proficiency Evaluation Manual, Activities 1-3, pp. 22-24 Select an activity from *Capítulo 4* to include in the *Somos así* Portfolio Assessment. Suggestion: Checklist appropriate items on appendices F, G, H, I and J, as needed.

Notes

Capítulo 5, lecciones 9 y 10

Day 1

Textbook	Support Materials
Warm-up: Review *los pronombres y adjetivos posesivos,* pp. 172 and 174	AC/CD: *¿Dónde estuvieron Uds. anoche?* (Side A, track 1)
Review the test on *Lección 8*	Quiz/Listening Activity 1, p. L35 (Side B, track 15)
Chapter preview: Discuss chapter opener, pp. 184-185	Transparency 36
¿Dónde estuvieron Uds. anoche?, p. 186	AC/CD: Activities 1-2 (Side A, tracks 2-3)
Activities 1-2, p. 187	

Notes

Day 2

Textbook	Support Materials
Warm-up: Review the dialog *¿Dónde estuvieron Uds. anoche?,* p. 186	AC/CD: *Cuba: El Caribe a todo sol* (Side A, track 4)
Conexión cultural, p. 188	Quiz/Listening Activity 2, p. L35 (Side B, track 16)
Activity 3, p. 189	Workbook Activity 1, p. 87
Repaso rápido, p. 189	Quiz/Listening Activity 3, p. L36 (Side B, track 17)
Activities 4-5, p. 190	Workbook Activities 2-4, pp. 88-89
Para ti: El pretérito de conocer, p. 190	Quiz/Written Activity 1, p. W49

Notes

Day 3

Textbook	Support Materials
Warm-up: Review *El pretérito*, p.189 Activity 6, p. 191 *Idioma*, p. 191 Activities 7-11, pp. 192-193 *Algo más*, p. 193 Activity 12, p. 194	AC/CD: Activity 6 (Side A, track 5) Quiz/Listening Activity 4, p. L36 (Side B, track 18) Workbook Activities 5-6, pp. 90-91 Quiz/Written Activity 2, p. W50 Quiz/Listening Activity 5, p. L37 (Side B, track 19) Workbook Activity 7, p. 92 Quiz/Written Activity 3, p. W51

Notes

Day 4

Textbook	Support Materials
Warm-up: Review *El pretérito y el imperfecto*, p. 191 *¿Qué compraron?*, p. 194 Activities 13-15, p. 195 *Para ti: Más comida en el supermercado*, p. 195	AC/CD: *¿Qué compraron?* (Side B, tracks 6-7) Transparencies 37-38 AC/CD: Activities 13-14 (Side B, tracks 8-9)

Notes

Day 5

Textbook	Support Materials
Warm-up: Review dialog *¿Qué compraron?*, p. 194	AC/CD: Activity 16 (Side B, track 10)
Idioma, p. 196	Workbook Activities 8-9, pp. 92-93
Estrategia, p. 196	Quiz/Written Activity 4, p. W52
Activities 16-17, pp. 196-197	AC/CD: Activity 17 (Side B, track 11)
Para ti: Los grados centígrados, p. 197	Quiz/Written Activity 5, p. W53
Conexión cultural, p. 197	AC/CD: Activity 18 (Side B, track 12)
Activity 18, p. 198	

Notes

Day 6

Textbook	Support Materials
Warm-up: Review *El presente de los verbos reír* and *freír,* p. 196	Quiz/Listening Activity 6, p. L37 (Side B, track 20)
Idioma, p. 198	Workbook Activities 10-11, pp. 94-95
Activities 19-23, pp. 199-201	Quiz/Written Activity 6, p. W54
	AC/CD: Activity 20 (Side B, track 13)

Notes

Day 7

Textbook	Support Materials
Warm-up: Review the uses of the preterite vs. the imperfect *El menú,* p. 201 Activities 24-25, p. 202 *Para ti: Más palabras en el menú,* p. 202 *Oportunidades,* p. 203 Activities 26-28, pp. 203-205	Quiz/Listening Activity 7, p. L38 (Side B, track 21) Transparency 39 Workbook Activities 12-13, pp. 95-96 Quiz/Written Activity 7, pp. W55-W56

Notes

Day 8

Textbook	Support Materials
Warm-up: Review food and menu vocabulary *Autoevaluación,* p. 205 *¡La práctica hace al maestro!,* Activities A-B, p. 206 Review for the test on *Lección 9*	Workbook Activity 14, p. 96 Oral Proficiency Evaluation Manual, Activities 1-3, pp. 25-27 Select and Activity from *Capítulo 5* to include in the *Somos así* Portfolio Assessment. Suggestion: Activity 22, p. 200, Appendices B-1 and F-1

Notes

Textbook	Support Materials
Test on *Lección 9*	Student Test Booklet, Activities 1-14, pp. 65-72
	Test Booklet Teacher's Edition, pp. 22-25
	Audiocassette/Audio CD listening comprehension test (Side A, tracks 9-12)
	Oral Proficiency Evaluation Manual, Activities 1-3, pp. 25-27
	Select and Activity from *Capítulo 5* to include in the *Somos así* Portfolio Assessment.
	Suggestion: Activity 22, p. 200, Appendices B and F

Notes

Textbook	Support Materials
Warm-up: Review irregular preterite forms, p. 198	AC/CD: *Buscando un vestido* (Side A, track 1)
Review the test on *Lección 9*	AC/CD: Activities 1-2 (Side A, tracks 2-3)
Buscando un vestido, p. 208	Quiz/Listening Activity 1, p. L39 (Side B, track 22)
Activities 1-2, p. 208	Transparency 40
Para ti: Expresiones adicionales, p. 208	Workbook Activity 1, p. 97
Conexión cultural, p. 209	AC/CD: *El Caribe* (Side A, track 4)
Activity 3, p. 210	Quiz/Listening Activity 2, p. L39 (Side B, track 23)
	Workbook Activity 2, p. 97

Notes

Day 11

Textbook	Support Materials
Warm-up: Review the dialog *Buscando un vestido,* p.208 *Oportunidades,* p. 210 *Idioma,* p. 210 Activities 4-6, pp. 211-212	Quiz/Listening Activity 3, p. L40 (Side B, track 24) Workbook Activities 3-4, pp. 98-99 Quiz/Written Activity 1, p. W57 AC/CD: Activity 4 (Side A, track 5)

Notes

Day 12

Textbook	Support Materials
Warm-up: Review *El imperfecto progresivo,* p. 210 *Algo más,* p. 212 Activities 7-9, pp. 213-214 *Buscando un vestido (continuación),* pp. 214-215 Activities 10-11, p. 215 *Para ti: Más palabras en la joyería,* p. 215	Workbook Activities 5-6, pp. 100-101 AC/CD: Activities 7-8 (Side A, tracks 6-7) AC/CD: *Buscando un vestido (continuación)* (Side B, track 8) Quiz/Listening Activity 4, p. L41 (Side B, track 25) Workbook Activity 7, p. 102 AC/CD: Activities 10-11 (Side B, tracks 9-10)

Notes

Day 13

Textbook	Support Materials
Warm-up: Review the dialog *Buscando un vestido (continuación)*, pp. 214-215	Quiz/Written Activity 2, p. W58
Algo más, p. 215	Workbook Activity 8, p. 103
Activities 12-13, p. 216	Quiz/Written Activity 3, p. W59
Idioma, p. 216	
Activities 14-16, pp. 217-218	

Notes

Day 14

Textbook	Support Materials
Warm-up: Review *Los adverbios terminados en –mente*, p. 216	AC/CD: *La cena elegante* (Side B, track 11)
La cena elegante, p. 218	Quiz/Written Activity 4, p. W59
Activities 17-18, p. 219	AC/CD: Activities 17-18 (Side B, tracks 12-13)
Repaso rápido, p. 219	Workbook Activity 9, p. 104
Activity 19, p. 220	Quiz/Written Activity 5, p. W60

Notes

Day 15

Textbook	Support Materials
Warm-up: Review the dialog *La cena elegante*, p. 218 *La cena elegante (continuación)*, p. 220 Activities 20-21, pp.220-221 *Para ti: Proverbios y dichos*, p. 221	AC/CD: *La cena elegante (continuación)* (Side B, track 14) Quiz/Listening Activity 5, p. L42 (Side B, track 26) Transparencies 41-42 Workbook Activity 10, p. 104 AC/CD: Activity 21 (Side B, track 15)

Notes

Day 16

Textbook	Support Materials
Warm-up: *Repaso rápido*, p. 219 *Idioma*, p. 221 Activities 22-24, pp. 222-223 *Autoevaluación*, p. 223	Quiz/Listening Activity 6, p. L43 (Side B, track 27) Workbook Activity 11, p. 105 Quiz/Written Activity 6, p. W61 AC/CD: Activity 24 (Side B, track 16)

Notes

Day 17	Textbook	Support Materials

Warm-up: Review the present and the imperfect progressive tenses
¡La práctica hace al maestro!, Activities A-B, p. 224
A leer, Activities A-B, pp. 226-227

Workbook Activity 12, p. 106
AC/CD: *El Caribe* (Side B, track 17)
Quiz/Listening Activity 7, p. L44 (Side B, track 28)
Quiz/Written Activity 7, p. W62

Notes

Day 18	Textbook	Support Materials

Warm-up: Review *Vocabulario,* p. 225
A escribir, p. 228
Review for the test on *Lección 10*

Video program, Episode 5
Oral Proficiency Evaluation Manual, Activities 1-3, pp. 28-30
Select an activity from *Capítulo 5* to include in the *Somos así* Portfolio Assessment. Suggestion: Checklist appropriate items on appendices F, G, H, I and J, as needed.

Notes

Day 19	Textbook	Support Materials
	Test on *Lección 10*	Student Test Booklet, Activities 1-12, pp. 73-80 Test Booklet Teacher's Edition, pp. 25-28 Audiocassette/Audio CD listening comprehension test (Side A, tracks 13-16) Oral Proficiency Evaluation Manual, Activities 1-3, pp. 28-30 Select an activity from *Capítulo 5* to include in the *Somos así* Portfolio Assessment. Suggestion: Checklist appropriate items on appendices F, G, H, I and J, as needed.

Notes

Day 20	Textbook	Support Materials
	Achievement Test 1	Student Test Booklet, Activities 1-28, pp. 81-94 Test Booklet Teacher's Edition, pp. 28-33 Audiocassette/Audio CD listening comprehension test (Side B, tracks 17-27) Oral Proficiency Evaluation Manual, Activities 1-5, pp. 31-34 Select an activity from *Capítulos 1-5* to include in the *Somos así* Portfolio Assessment. Suggestion: Checklist appropriate items on appendices C, D, E, F, G, H, I and J, as needed.

Notes

Capítulo 6, lecciones 11 y 12

Day 1

Textbook	Support Materials
Warm-up: Have students report about a past action or event Review the test on *Lección 10* Review the Achievement Test 1 Chapter preview: Discuss chapter opener, pp. 230-231 *En casa de Felipe*, p. 23 Activities 1-3, p. 233 *Para ti: Los quehaceres,* p. 233	AC/CD: *En casa de Felipe* (Side A, track 1) Transparency 43 AC/CD: Activities 1-2 (Side A, tracks 2-3) Quiz/Listening Activity 1, p. L45 (Side A, track 1) Quiz/Written Activity 2, p. W63

Notes

Day 2

Textbook	Support Materials
Warm-up: Review *Los quehaceres,* p. 233 *Conexión cultural,* p. 234 Activity 4, p. 235 *Idioma,* pp. 235-236 Activity 5, p. 236	AC/CD: *Bolivia* (Side A, track 4) Quiz/Listening Activity 2, p. L46 (Side A, track 2) Workbook Activity 1, p. 107 AC/CD: Activity 4 (Side A, track 5) Quiz/Listening Activity 3, p. L46 (Side A, track 3) Quiz/Written Activity 2, p. W64

Notes

Day 3

Textbook	Support Materials
Warm-up: Review *El subjuntivo*, pp. 235-236	Workbook Activity 2, p. 108
Activity 6, p. 237	Quiz/Written Activity 3, p. W65
Algo más, p. 237	AC/CD: Activities 8-9 (Side A, tracks 6-7)
Activities 7-9, pp. 238-239	

Notes

Day 4

Textbook	Support Materials
Warm-up: Review *El subjuntivo con mandatos indirectos*, p. 237	Workbook Activities 3-4, pp. 109-110
Idioma, p. 239	Quiz/Written Activity 4, p. W66
Activities 10-12, p. 240	AC/CD: *En la casa de Felipe (continuación)* (Side A, track 8)
En casa de Felipe (continuación), p. 241	AC/CD: Activity 13 (Side A, track 9)
Activity 13, p. 241	

Notes

Textbook	Support Materials
Warm-up: Review dialog *En la casa de Felipe (continuación)*, p. 241	Quiz/Listening Activity 4, p. L47 (Side A, track 4)
Algo más, p. 242	Workbook Activity 5, p. 111
Activity 14, p. 242	Quiz/Listening Activity 5, p. L48 (Side A, track 5)
Para ti: Palabras de cariño, p. 242	Workbook Activities 6-7, pp. 111-112
Idioma, p. 243	
Activities 15-16, p. 243	

Notes

Textbook	Support Materials
Warm-up: Review *Verbos irregulares en el subjuntivo*, p. 243	AC/CD: Activity 17 (Side A, track 10)
Activity 17, p. 244	AC/CD: *Trabajando en casa* (Side B tracks 11-12)
Trabajando en casa, p. 245	AC/CD: Activity 18 (Side B, track 13)
Activity 18, p. 245	Quiz/Listening Activity 6, p. L48 (Side A, track 6)
	Transparency 44
	Workbook Activity 8, p. 112

Notes

Day 7	**Textbook**	**Support Materials**

Warm-up: Review dialog *Trabajando en casa,* p. 245
Activity 19, p. 246
Algo más, p. 246
Activities 20-22, pp. 246-247
Trabajando en casa (continuación), p. 248
Activity 23, p. 248

AC/CD: Activity 19 (Side B, track 14)
Workbook Activity 9, p. 113
Quiz/Written Activity 5, p. W67
AC/CD: *Trabajando en casa (continuación)* (Side B, track 15)
AC/CD: Activity 23 (Side B, track 16)

Notes

Day 8	**Textbook**	**Support Materials**

Warm-up: Review *Más sobre el subjuntivo con mandatos indirectos,* p. 246
Algo más, p. 248
Activities 24-25, p. 249
En la casa, p. 250
Activity 26, p. 250

Workbook Activity 10, p. 114
Quiz/Written Activity 6, p. W67
AC/CD: Activity 24 (Side B, track 17)
AC/CD: *En la casa* (Side B, track 18)
Quiz/Listening Activity 7, p. L49 (Side A, track 7)
Transparencies 45-46
Workbook Activity 11, p. 115
Quiz/Written Activity 7, p. W68

Notes

Day 9

Textbook	Support Materials
Warm-up: Review vocabulary from *En la casa*, p. 250	AC/CD: Activity 27 (Side B, track 19)
Activities 27-28, p. 251	Transparency 47
Para ti: La arquitectura hispana, p. 251	Workbook Activity 12, p. 160
Autoevaluación, p. 251	Oral Proficiency Evaluation Manual, Activities 1-3, pp. 35-37
¡La práctica hace al maestro!, Activities A-B, p. 252	Select an activity from *Capítulo 6* to include in the *Somos así* Portfolio Assessment.
Review for the test on *Lección 11*	Suggestion: Activity B, p. 252, Appendices B-1 and F-1

Notes

Day 10

Textbook	Support Materials
Test on *Lección* 11	Student Test Booklet, Activities 1-13, pp. 95-102
	Test Booklet Teacher's Edition, pp. 34-36
	Audiocassette/Audio CD listening comprehension test (Side A, tracks 1-4)
	Oral Proficiency Evaluation Manual, Activities 1-3, pp. 35-37
	Select an activity from *Capítulo 6* to include in the *Somos así* Portfolio Assessment. Suggestion: Activity B, p. 252, Appendices B-1 and F-1

Notes

Textbook	Support Materials
Warm-up: Review house and family vocabulary	AC/CD: *Las reglas de la casa* (Side A, tracks 1-2)
Review the test on *Lección 11*	Quiz/Listening Activity 1, p. L51 (Side A. track 8)
Las reglas de la casa, p. 254	AC/CD: Activities 1-2 (Side A, tracks 3-4)
Activities 1-2, p. 255	
Estrategia, p. 255	

Notes

Textbook	Support Materials
Warm-up: Review the dialog *Las reglas de la casa,* p. 254, and discuss rules at home,	AC/CD: *Los países bolivianos* (Side A, track 5)
Conexión cultural, p. 256	Quiz/Listening Activity 2, p. L51 (Side A, track 9)
Activity 3, p. 257	Workbook Activities 1-3, pp. 117-119
Idioma, p. 257	Quiz/Written Activity 1, p. W69

Notes

Day 13

Textbook	Support Materials
Warm-up: Review *El subjuntivo con verbos de emoción y duda,* p. 257	AC/CD: Activities 4 and 8 (Side A, tracks 6-7)
Activities 4-7, pp. 258-259	Workbook Activities 4-5, pp. 120-121
Algo más, p. 260	Quiz/Written Activity 2, p. W70
Activity 8, p. 260	

Notes

Day 14

Textbook	Support Materials
Warm-up: Review *Otros verbos de emoción,* p. 260	Quiz/Listening Activity 3, p. L52 (Side A, track 10)
Activities 9-10, p. 261	Workbook Activities 6-7, pp. 122-123
Algo más, p. 262	Quiz/Written Activity 3, p. W71
Activities 11-12, p. 263	AC/CD: Activity 12 (Side A, track 8)
Para ti: Proverbios y dichos, p. 263	

Notes

Day 15	Textbook	Support Materials
	Warm-up: Review *El subjuntivo con expresiones impersonales* Activities 13-14, p. 264 *La abuela cumple años,* p. 265 Activity 15, p. 266	AC/CD: *La abuela cumple años* (Side B, track 9) Quiz/Listening Activity 4, p. L52 (Side A, track 11) AC/CD: Activity 15 (Side B, track 10)

Notes

Day 16	Textbook	Support Materials
	Warm-up: Review the dialog *La abuela cumple años,* p. 265 Activities 16-17, p. 266 *Algunos aparatos de la casa,* p. 266	AC/CD: Activity 16 (Side B, track 12) AC/CD: *Algunos aparatos de la casa* (Side B, track 12) Quiz/Listening Activity 5, p. L53 (Side A, track 12) Transparencies 48-49 Workbook Activities 8-9, pp. 124-125 Quiz/Written Activity 4, p. W72

Notes

Day 17

Textbook	Support Materials
Warm-up: Review *Algunos aparatos de la casa*, p. 266 *Para ti: Otros aparatos de la casa*, p. 267 Activity 18, p. 267 *Oportunidades*, p. 267 Activity 19, p. 268	AC/CD: Activity 18 (Side B, track 13) Quiz/Written Activity 5, p. W73 Video program, Episode 6

Notes

Day 18

Textbook	Support Materials
Warm-up: Review express your opinions or doubts about an upcoming event Activities 20-21, p. 269 *Autoevaluación*, p. 269 *¡La práctica hace al maestro!* Activities A-B, p. 270 *A escribir*, p. 276	Workbook Activity 10, p. 126 Quiz/Listening Activity 6, p. L53 (Side A, track 13)

Notes

Textbook	Support Materials
Warm-up: Review *Vocabulario,* p. 271 *A leer,* Activities A-B, pp. 272-275 Review for the test on *Lección 12*	AC/CD: *La familia hispana* (Side B, track 14) Quiz/Listening Activity 7, p. L54 (Side A, track 14) Quiz/Written Activity 6, p. W74 AC/CD: Activities A-B (Side B, tracks 15-16) Oral Proficiency Evaluation Manual, Activities 1-3, pp.38-40 Select an activity from *Capítulo 6* to include in the *Somos así* Portfolio Assessment. Suggestion: Checklist appropriate items on appendices C, D, E, F, G, H, I and J, as needed.

Notes

Textbook	Support Materials
Test on *Lección 12*	Student Test Booklet, Activities 1-12, pp. 103-110 Test Booklet Teacher's Edition, pp. 36-39 Audiocassette/Audio CD listening comprehension test (Side A, tracks 5-8) Oral Proficiency Evaluation Manual, Activities 1-3, pp.38-40 Select an activity from *Capítulo 6* to include in the *Somos así* Portfolio Assessment. Suggestion: Checklist appropriate items on appendices C, D, E, F, G, H, I and J, as needed.

Notes

Capítulo 7, lecciones 13 y 14

Day 1

Textbook	Support Materials
Warm-up: Review expressions of doubt and emotion	AC/CD: *Las noticias* (Side A, track 1)
Review the test on *Lección 12*	AC/CD: Activity 1 (Side A, track 2)
Chapter preview: Discuss chapter opener, pp. 278-279	Quiz/Listening Activity 1, p. L55 (Side B, track 15)
Las noticias, p. 280	Transparency 50
Activity 1, p. 280	AC/CD: *El Uruguay* (Side A, track 3)
Conexión cultural, p. 281	Quiz/Listening Activity 2, p. L55 (Side B, track 16)
Activity 2, p. 282	Workbook Activity 1, p. 127

Notes

Day 2

Textbook	Support Materials
Warm-up: Review the dialog *Las noticias*, p. 280	AC/CD: *Las noticias (continuación)* (Side A, track 4)
Las noticias (continuación), p. 282	AC/CD: Activities 3-4 (Side A, tracks 5-6)
Activity 3, p. 283	Quiz/Listening Activity 3, p. L56 (Side B, track 17)
Algo más, p. 283	Workbook Activity 2, p. 128
Activity 4, p. 283	Quiz/Written Activity 1, p. W75
Para ti: Más sobre las noticias, p. 283	

Notes

Day 3	**Textbook**	**Support Materials**

Warm-up: Review *Para hablar de las noticias* and *Más sobre las noticias,* p. 283
Oportunidades, p. 284
Activities 5-6, pp. 284-285
Idioma, p. 285
Activity 7, p. 286

Quiz/Listening Activity 4, p. L56 (Side B, track 18)
Workbook Activities 3-5, pp. 129-131
Quizzes/Written Activities 2-3, p. W76

Notes

Day 4	**Textbook**	**Support Materials**

Warm-up: Review *El pretérito perfecto y el participio,* p. 285
Activities 8-10, pp. 286-287
Para ti: Proverbios y dichos, p. 287
Activity 11, p. 288
Algo más, p. 288

AC/CD: Activities 10-11 (Side A, tracks 7-8)
Quiz/Listening Activity 5, p. L56 (Side B, track 19)
Workbook Activities 6-7, pp. 132-133
Quiz/Written Activity 4, p. W77

Notes

Day 5	**Textbook**	**Support Materials**

Warm-up: Review *Participios irregulares*, p. 288
Activities 12-15, pp. 289-290
En la televisión, pp. 290-291
Activities 16-17, p. 291

AC/CD: *En la televisión* (Side B, track 9)
Quiz/Written Activity 5, pp. W78-W79
AC/CD: Activities 16-17 (Side B, tracks 10-11)

Notes

Day 6	**Textbook**	**Support Materials**

Warm-up: Review by discussing activities that students have done in the past
Algo más, p. 291
Activities 18-20, pp. 292-293
En la televisión (continuación), p. 293
Activity 21, p. 294

Workbook Activity 8, p. 134
Quiz/Written Activity 6, pp. W80-W81
AC/CD: Activity 20 (Side B, track 12)
AC/CD: *En la televisión (continuación)* (Side B, track 13)
Quiz/Listening Activity 6, p. L57 (Side B, track 20)
Workbook Activity 9, p. 135
AC/CD: Activity 21 (Side B, track 14)

Notes

Day 7

Textbook	Support Materials
Warm-up: Review the dialog *En la televisión (continuación)*, p. 293	AC/CD: Activity 22 (Side B, track 15)
Activity 22, p. 294	Quiz/Listening Activity 7, p. L58 (Side B, track 21)
Algo más, p. 295	Workbook Activity 10, p. 135
Activity 23, p. 295	Quiz/Written Activity 7, p. W82

Notes

Day 8

Textbook	Support Materials
Warm-up: Have students tell something exciting that they have done this year	Workbook Activity 11, p. 136
Activities 24-25, p. 296	Oral Proficiency Evaluation Manual, Activities 1-3, pp. 41-43
Autoevaluación, p. 297	Select an activity from *Capítulo 7* to include in the *Somos así* Portfolio Assessment.
Review *Vocabulario*, p. 299	Suggestion: Activity A, p. 298,
¡La práctica hace al maestro!, Activities A-B, p. 298	Appendices B-1 and F-1
Review for the test on *Lección 13*	

Notes

Day 9

Textbook	Support Materials
Test on *Lección 13*	Student Test Booklet, Activities 1-11, pp. 111-118 Test Booklet Teacher's Edition, pp. 39-41 Audiocassette/Audio CD listening comprehension test (Side A, tracks 9-12) Oral Proficiency Evaluation Manual, Activities 1-3, pp. 41-43 Select an activity from *Capítulo 7* to include in the *Somos así* Portfolio Assessment. Suggestion: Activity A, p. 298, Appendices B-1 and F-1

Notes

Day 10

Textbook	Support Materials
Warm-up: Review *El participio como adjetivo*, p. 295 Review the test on *Lección 13* *En el periódico*, p. 300 Activity 1, p. 301 *Algo más*, p. 301 Activities 2-3, p. 301 *Para ti: Más palabras de los periódicos*, p. 301	AC/CD: *En el periódico* (Side A, track 1) Quiz/Listening Activity 1, p. L59 (Side B, track 22 AC/CD: Activities 1-2 (Side A, tracks 2-3) Transparency 51 Workbook Activity 1, p. 137 Quiz/Written Activity 1, p. W83

Notes

Textbook	Support Materials
Warm-up: Review the dialog *En el periódico*, p. 300 *Oportunidades*, p. 302 Activities 4-5, p. 302 *Conexión cultural*, p. 303 Activity 6, p. 304	AC/CD: *El Paraguay* (Side A, track 4) Quiz/Listening Activity 2, p. L59 (Side B, track 23) Workbook Activity 2, p. 138

Notes

Textbook	Support Materials
Warm-up: Have students identify the sections of newspapers and magazines in Spanish *Idioma*, p. 304 Activities 7-11, pp. 304-306	Quiz/Listening Activity 3, p. L60 (Side B, track 24) Workbook Activities 3-4, pp. 139-140 Quiz/Written Activity 2, p. W84

Notes

Day 13

Textbook	Support Materials
Warm-up: Review *El pretérito pluscuamperfecto*, p. 304	AC/CD: *Las noticias se escuchan por Radio Ñandutí* (Side A track 5)
Activity 12, p. 307	Quiz/Listening Activity 4, p. L61 (Side B, track 25)
Las noticias se escuchan por Radio Ñandutí, p. 307	Workbook Activity 5, p. 141
Activities 13-14, p. 308	AC/CD: Activity 13-14 (Side A, tracks 6-7)

Notes

Day 14

Textbook	Support Materials
Warm-up: Review the dialog *Las noticias se escuchan por Radio Ñandutí,* p. 307	Quiz/Listening Activity 5, p. L62 (Side B, track 26)
Estrategia, p. 308	Workbook Activity 6, p. 142
Activity 15, p. 309	Quiz/Written Activity 3, p. W85
Repaso rápido, p. 309	AC/CD: Activities 15-16 (Side A, tracks 8-9)
Activity 16, p. 309	Quiz/Written Activity 4, p. W86

Notes

Day 15

Textbook	Support Materials
Warm-up: Review *La voz pasiva,* p. 309 *Idioma,* p. 310 Activities 17-19, pp. 310-311	AC/CD: Activity 17 (Side B, track 10) Quiz/Listening Activity 6, p. L63 (Side B, track 27) Workbook Activities 7-8, pp. 143-144 Quiz/Written Activity 5, p. W87

Notes

Day 16

Textbook	Support Materials
Warm-up: Review *La voz pasiva: un poco más,* p. 310 Activity 20, p. 312 *El fútbol,* p. 312 *Algo más,* p. 313 Activities 21-22, p. 313	AC/CD: Activity 20 (Side B, track 11) AC/CD: *El fútbol* (Side B, track 12) Transparencies 52-53 AC/CD: Activity 21 (Side B, track 13) Workbook Activity 9, p. 145 Quiz/Written Activity 6, p. W88

Notes

Day 17	Textbook	Support Materials
	Warm-up: Review *El fútbol*, pp. 312-313 *Autoevaluación*, p. 313 *¡La práctica hace al maestro!* Activities A-B, p. 314	Workbook Activity 10, p. 146

Notes

Day 18	Textbook	Support Materials

	Warm-up: Review *Vocabulario*, p. 315
	A leer, Activities A-B, pp. 316-319
		Quiz/Listening Activity 7, p. L64 (Side B,
		    track 28)
		Quiz/Written Activity 7, p. W89
		AC/CD: *Ayuda para las víctimas del*
		    terremoto (Side B, track 14)
		AC/CD: Activities A-B (Side B, tracks
		    15-16)

Notes

Day 19	**Textbook**	**Support Materials**

Warm-up: *Repaso,* p. 321
A escribir, p. 320
Review for the test on *Lección 14*

Video Program, Episode 7
Oral Proficiency Evaluation Manual,
   Activities 1-3, pp. 44-46
Select an activity from *Capítulo 7* to include
   in the *Somos así* Portfolio Assessment.
   Suggestion: Checklist appropriate items
   on appendices C, D, E, F, G, H, I and J,
   as needed.

Notes

Day 20	**Textbook**	**Support Materials**

Test on *Lección 14*

Student Test Booklet, Activities 1-12,
   pp. 119-126
Test booklet Teacher's Edition, pp. 41-44
Audiocassette/Audio CD listening
   comprehension test (Side A, tracks 13-16)
Oral Proficiency Evaluation Manual,
   Activities 1-3, pp. 44-46
Select an activity from *Capítulo 7* to include
   in the *Somos así* Portfolio Assessment.
   Suggestion: Checklist appropriate items
   on appendices C, D, E, F, G, H, I and J,
   as needed.

Notes

Capítulo 8, lecciones 15 y 16

Day 1

Textbook	Support Materials
Warm-up: Review *La voz pasiva*, p. 310	AC/CD: *Las próximas vacaciones* (Side A, track 1)
Review the test on *Lección 14*	
Chapter preview: Discuss the chapter opener, pp. 322-323	Quiz/Listening Activity 1, p. L65 (Side A. track 1)
Las próximas vacaciones, p. 324	Transparency 54
Activity 1, p. 325	AC/CD: Activity 1 (Side A, track 2)
Para ti: La corrida de toros, p. 325	AC/CD: *La tortilla española* (Side A, track 3)
Conexión cultural, p. 325	
Activity 2, p. 326	Quiz/Listening Activity 2, p. L65 (Side A, track 2)
	Workbook Activity 1, p. 147

Notes

Day 2

Textbook	Support Materials
Warm-up: Review dialog *Las próximas vacaciones*, p. 324	AC/CD: *Las próximas vacaciones (continuación)* (Side A, tracks 4-5)
Las próximas vacaciones (continuación), p. 326	Workbook Activity 2, p. 148
Activities 3-4, p. 327	Quiz/Written Activity 1, p. W91
Repaso rápido, p. 327	AC/CD: Activities 3-5 (Side A, tracks 6-8)
Activity 5, p. 327	Quiz/Written Activity 2, p. W92

Notes

Day 3

Textbook	Support Materials
Warm-up: Review *El futuro con ir a*, p. 327 Activity 6, p. 328 *Idioma*, p. 328 Activities 7-11, pp. 329-330	Quiz/Listening Activity 3, p. L66 (Side A, track 3) Workbook Activities 3-5, pp. 149-151 Quizzes/Written Activities 3-4, pp. W93-W94 AC/CD: Activities 7, 9 and 10 (Side A, tracks 9-11)

Notes

Day 4

Textbook	Support Materials
Warm-up: Have students tell what they will do next weekend *Algo más*, p. 331 Activities 12-14, pp. 331-332	AC/CD: Activity 12 (Side B, track 12) Quiz/Listening Activity 4, p. L66 (Side A, track 4) Workbook Activity 6, p. 152 AC/CD: Activity 13 (Side B, track 13)

Notes

Day 5

Textbook	Support Materials
Warm-up: Review *El futuro de probabilidad,* p. 331	AC/CD: *Las reservaciones* (Side B, tracks 14-15)
Las reservaciones, p. 333	Quiz/Listening Activity 5, p. L67 (Side A, track 5)
Activities 15-16, p. 334	Workbook Activity 7, p. 153
Para ti: Otra palabras y expresiones, p. 334	AC/CD: Activities 15-16 (Side B, tracks 16-17)
Algo más, p. 335	Workbook Activity 8, p. 154
Activities 17-18, p. 335	Quiz/Written Activity 5, p. W95

Notes

Day 6

Textbook	Support Materials
Warm-up: Review *El futuro: los verbos reflexivos,* p. 335	Quiz/Listening Activity 6, p. L67 (Side A, track 6)
Idioma, p. 336	Workbook Activities 9-10, pp. 155-156
Activities 19-22, pp. 337-338	Quizzes/Written Activities 6-7, pp. W95-W96
	AC/CD: Activity 20 (Side B, track 18)

Notes

Textbook	Support Materials
Warm-up: Review *El futuro de los verbos irregulares,* p. 336 *Oportunidades,* p. 339 Activity 23, p. 339 *En la agencia de viajes,* p. 340 Activities 24-26, pp. 340-341	Quiz/Listening Activity 7, p. L68 (Side A, track 7) Workbook Activity 11, p. 157 AC/CD: Activity 25 (Side B, track 19)

Notes

Textbook	Support Materials
Warm-up: Review *Vocabulario,* p. 343 *Autoevaluación,* p. 341 *¡La práctica hace al maestro!,* Activities A-B, p. 342 Review for the test on *Lección 15*	Workbook Activity 12, p. 158 Oral Proficiency Evaluation Manual, Activities 1-3, pp. 47-49 Select an activity from *Capítulo 8* to include in the *Somos así* Portfolio Assessment. Suggestion: Activity 11, p. 330, Appendices B-1 and F-1

Notes

Day 9

Textbook	Support Materials
Test on *Lección 15*	Student Test Booklet, Activities 1-13, pp. 127-134
	Test Booklet Teacher's Edition, pp. 44-46
	Audiocassette/Audio CD listening comprehension test (Side B, tracks 17-20)
	Oral Proficiency Evaluation Manual, Activities 1-3, pp. 47-49
	Select an activity from *Capítulo 8* to include in the *Somos así* Portfolio Assessment. Suggestion: Activity 11, p. 330, Appendices B-1 and F-1

Notes

Day 10

Textbook	Support Materials
Warm-up: Have students tell what their daily routines will be during summer vacation	AC/CD: *En el mostrador de la aerolínea* (Side A, tracks 1-2)
Review the test on *Lección 15*	Quiz/Listening Activity 1, p. L69 (Side A, track 8)
En el mostrador de la aerolínea, p. 344	Transparency 55
Activities 1-2, pp. 344-345	Workbook Activity 1, p. 159
Algo más, p. 345	AC/CD: Activities 1-2 (Side A, tracks 3-4)
Activity 3, p. 345	Quiz/Listening Activity 2, p. L70 (Side A, track 9)
	Transparency 56
	Quiz/Written Activity 1, pp. W97-W98

Notes

Day 11 | **Textbook** | **Support Materials**

Warm-up: Review the dialog *En el mostrador de la aerolínea,* p. 344
Activity 4, p. 346
Oportunidades, p. 346
Conexión cultural, p. 347
Activity 5, p. 348

AC/CD: *España* (Side A, track 5)
Quiz/Listening Activity 3, p. L71 (Side A, track 10)
Workbook Activity 2, p. 160
Quiz/Listening Activity 4, p. L71 (Side A, track 11)

Notes

Day 12 | **Textbook** | **Support Materials**

Warm-up: Review *España,* p. 347
Idioma, p. 348
Activities 6-9, pp. 349-350
Para ti: Proverbios y dichos, p. 350
Activity 10, p. 351

AC/CD: Activities 7-8 (Side A, tracks 6-7)

Notes

Textbook	**Support Materials**

Warm-up: Review *El condicional*, p. 348
Bienvenidos a su vuelo número 108, p. 351
Activity 11, p. 352
Algo más, p. 352
Activities 12-13, p. 353

AC/CD: *Bienvenidos a su vuelo número 108*
  (Side A, track 8)
Quiz/Listening Activity 5, p. L72
Workbook Activities 5-7, pp. 163-165
Quiz/Written Activity 4, pp. W100-W101
AC/CD: Activity 12 (Side A, track 9)

Notes

Textbook	**Support Materials**

Warm-up: Review *El condicional de los verbos*
  irregulares, p. 352
Activity 14, p. 354
En taxi al hotel, p. 354
Activities 15-16, pp. 354-355
Para ti: ¿A qué hora?, p. 355
En la recepción del hotel, p. 355
Activity 11, p. 356

AC/CD: *En taxi al hotel* (Side A, track 10)
AC/CD): Activities 15-16 (Side A, tracks
  11-12)
AC/CD): *En la recepción del hotel* (Side A,
  tracks 13-14)
Quiz/Listening Activity 6, p. L73 (Side A,
  track 13)
Workbook Activity 8, p. 166
AC/CD: Activity 17 (Side A, track 15)

Notes

Day 15

Textbook	Support Materials
Warm-up: Review the dialogs *En taxi al hotel*, p. 354, and *En la recepción del hotel*, p. 355 *Algo más*, p. 356 Activity 18, p. 356 *Oportunidades*, p. 357 Activity 19, p. 357 *Conexión cultural*, p. 358 Activity 20, p. 359	AC/CD: Activity 18 (Side B, track 16) Quiz/Written Activity 5, p. W102

Notes

Day 16

Textbook	Support Materials
Warm-up: Have students describe what would be their ideal hotel. Activity 21, p. 359 *Algo más*, p. 360 Activities 22-23, pp. 360-361	Workbook Activity 9, p. 167 Quiz/Written Activity 6, p. W103 AC/CD: Activities 22-23 (Side B, tracks 17-18)

Notes

Day 17 | **Textbook** | **Support Materials**

Warm-up: Review *El condicional de probabilidad*, p. 360
Autoevaluación, p. 361
¡La práctica hace al maestro! Activities A-B, p. 362

Workbook Activity 10, p. 168

Notes

Day 18 | **Textbook** | **Support Materials**

Warm-up: Review *Vocabulario*, p. 363
A leer: Activities A-B, pp. 364-369

Quiz/Listening Activity 7, p. L74 (Side A, track 14)
AC/CD: *Lázaro cuenta su vida y de quien fue hijo* (Side B, track 19)
AC/CD: Activities A-B (Side B, tracks 20-21)
Quiz/Written Activity 7, p. W104

Notes

Day 19

Textbook	Support Materials

Warm-up: Review *Repaso*, p. 371
A escribir, p. 370
Review for the test on *Lección 16*
	Video Program, Episode 8
	Oral Proficiency Evaluation Manual,
	    Activities 1-3, pp. 50-52
	Select an activity from *Capítulo 8* to include
	    in the *Somos así* Portfolio Assessment.
	    Suggestion: Checklist appropriate items
	    on appendices C, D, E, F, G, H, I and J,
	    as needed.

Notes

Day 20

Textbook	Support Materials

Test on *Lección 16*	Student Test Booklet, Activities 1-12,
	    pp. 135-142
	Test Booklet Teacher's Edition, pp. 47-49
	Audiocassette/Audio CD listening
	    comprehension test (Side B, tracks 21-24)
	Oral Proficiency Evaluation Manual,
	    Activities 1-3, pp. 50-52
	Select an activity from *Capítulo 8* to include
	    in the *Somos así* Portfolio Assessment.
	    Suggestion: Checklist appropriate items
	    on appendices C, D, E, F, G, H, I and J,
	    as needed.

Notes

Capítulo 9, lecciones 17 y 18

Day 1

Textbook	Support Materials
Warm-up: Review *El condicional de probabilidad*, p. 360 Review the test on *Lección 16* Chapter preview: Discuss chapter opener pp. 372-373 *Asistir a la universidad*, p. 374 Activities 1-2, p. 375 *Oportunidades*, p. 375	AC/CD: *Asistir a la universidad* (Side A, tracks 1-2) Quiz/Listening Activity 1, p. L75 (Side B, track 15) AC/CD: Activities 1-2 (Side A, tracks 3-4)

Notes

Day 2

Textbook	Support Materials
Warm-up: Review the dialog *Asistir a la universidad*, p. 374 *Conexión cultural*, p. 376 Activity 3, p. 377 *Oportunidades*, p. 377 *Los empleos*, p. 378	AC/CD: *Los empleos* (Side A, track 5) Transparencies 57-58 Quiz/Listening Activity 2, p. L76 (Side B, track 16)

Notes

Day 3

Textbook	Support Materials
Warm-up: Review *Los empleos,* p. 378 *Algo más,* p. 378 *Para ti: Más empleos,* p. 378 Activities 4-5, p. 379	Quiz/Listening Activity 3, p. L76 (Side B, track 17) Workbook Activities 1-2, pp. 169-170 Quizzes/Written Activities 1-2, pp. W105-W106 AC/CD: Activity 5 (Side B, track 6)

Notes

Day 4

Textbook	Support Materials
Warm-up: Review *Más sobre los empleos* and *Más empleos,* p. 378 Activities 6-10, pp. 380-381 *Repaso rápido,* p. 382 Activity 11, p. 382	Quiz/Listening Activity 4, p. L77 (Side B, track 18) Workbook Activities 3-4, pp. 171-172 Quiz/Written Activity 3, p. W107

Notes

Day 5

Textbook	Support Materials
Warm-up: Review *Los usos de **haber**,* p. 382 Activity 12, p. 383 *Idioma,* p. 383 Activities 13-16, pp. 384-385	AC/CD: Activity 12 (Side B, track 7) Quiz/Listening Activity 5, p. L77 (Side B, track 19) Workbook Activities 5-6, pp. 173-174 Quizzes/Written Activities 4-5, pp. W108-W109 AC/CD: Activity 13 (Side B, track 8)

Notes

Day 6

Textbook	Support Materials
Warm-up: Review *El pretérito perfecto del subjuntivo,* p. 383 Activities 17-18 p. 386 *Amigos por correspondencia,* p. 387 Activities 19-20, p. 388	Quiz/Listening Activity 6, p. L78 (Side B, track 20) Workbook Activity 7, p. 175 AC/CD: Activities 19-20 (Side B, tracks 9-10)

Notes

Day 7

Textbook	Support Materials
Warm-up: Review *Amigos por correspondencia*, p. 387 *Idioma*, pp. 388-389 Activities 21-25, pp. 389-391	Quiz/Listening Activity 7, p. L78 (Side B, track 21) Workbook Activities 8-9, pp. 176-177 Quizzes/Written Activities 6-7, p. W110

Notes

Day 8

Textbook	Support Materials
Warm-up: Review *Vocabulario*, p. 393 *Autoevaluación*, p. 391 *¡La práctica hace al maestro!*, Activities A-B, p. 392 Review for the test on *Lección 17*	Workbook Activity 10, p. 178 Oral Proficiency Evaluation Manual, Activities 1-3, pp. 53-55 Select an activity from *Capítulo 9* to include in the *Somos así* Portfolio Assessment. Suggestion: Activity 18, p. 386, Appendices B-1 and F-1

Notes

Day 9

Textbook	Support Materials
Test on *Lección 17*	Student Test Booklet, Activities 1-12, pp. 143-150 Test booklet Teacher's Edition, pp. 49-51 Audiocassette/Audio CD listening comprehension test (Side A, tracks 1-5) Oral Proficiency Evaluation Manual, Activities 1-3, pp. 53-55 Select an activity from *Capítulo 9* to include in the *Somos así* Portfolio Assessment. Suggestion: Activity 18, p. 386, Appendices B-1 and F-1

Notes

Day 10

Textbook	Support Materials
Warm-up: Review subjunctive phrases by having students talk about aspirations Review the test on *Lección 17* *¡Qué suerte tienes!*, p. 394 Activities 1-2, p. 395 *Estrategia*, p. 395	AC/CD: *¡Qué suerte tienes!* (Side A, track 1) Quiz/Listening Activity 1, p. L79 (Side B, track 22) Transparency 59 Workbook Activity 1, p. 179 AC/CD: Activities 1-2 (Side A, tracks 2-3)

Notes

Day 11

Textbook	Support Materials
Warm-up: Review dialog *¡Qué suerte tienes!,* p. 394	Quiz/Listening Activity 2, p. L79 (Side B, track 23)
Para ti: Proverbios y dichos, p. 396	Transparency 60
El lenguaje del cuerpo, p. 396	Workbook Activity 2, p. 180
Activity 3, p. 396	Quiz/Listening Activity 3, p. L80 (Side B, track 24)
Repaso rápido, p. 397	Workbook Activities 3-4, pp. 181-182
Activity 4, p. 397	Quiz/Written Activity 1, p. W111

Notes

Day 12

Textbook	Support Materials
Warm-up: Review *El lenguaje del cuerpo,* p. 396	Quiz/Listening Activity 4, p. L80 (Side B, track 25)
Activity 5, p. 398	Workbook Activities 5-7, pp. 183-186
Idioma, pp. 398-399	Quiz/Written Activity 2, p. W112
Activities 6-7, pp. 399-400	

Notes

Day 13

Textbook	Support Materials
Warm-up: Review *El subjuntivo: un resumen*, pp. 398-399 Activities 8-10, pp. 400-401	Quiz/Written Activity 3, p. W113 AC/CD: Activity 8 (Side A, track 4)

Notes

Day 14

Textbook	Support Materials
Warm-up: Review the geographical location of Spanish-speaking countries. *Conexión cultural,* pp. 402-403	Quiz/Listening Activity 5, p. L81 (Side B, track 26) Transparencies 61-62 Workbook Activity 8, pp. 187

Notes

Day 15

Textbook	Support Materials
Warm-up: Review *El mundo*, pp. 402-403 *Algo más*, p. 404 Para ti: Más países del mundo, p. 404 Activities 11-12, p. 405	Workbook Activity 9, pp. 188-189 Quiz/Listening Activity 6, p. L82 (Side B, track 27) Quizzes/Written Activities 4-5, pp. W114-W116 AC/CD: Activity 12 (Side A, track 5)

Notes

Day 16

Textbook	Support Materials
Warm-up: Review *Más países del mundo* and *Las nacionalidades*, pp. 404-405 Activities 13-17, pp. 406-407 *Autoevaluación*, p. 407	AC/CD: Activity 16 (Side A, track 6)

Notes

Textbook	Support Materials
Warm-up: Review *Vocabulario,* p. 409	Workbook Activity 10, p. 190
¡La práctica hace al maestro!, Activities A-B, p. 408	Quiz/Written Activity 6, p. W117
	Oral Proficiency Evaluation Manual, Activities 1-3, pp. 56-58

Notes

Day 18

Textbook	Support Materials
Warm-up: Review *Lázaro cuenta su vida y de quien fue hijo*, pp. 365-369	AC/CD: *Lázaro cuenta su vida y de quien fue hijo (continuación)* (Side B, track 7)
A leer, Activities A-B, pp. 410-417	AC/CD: Activities A-B (Side B, tracks 8-9)
	Quiz/Listening Activity 7, p. L82 (Side B, track 28)
	Quiz/Written Activity 7, p. W118

Notes

Day 19

Textbook	Support Materials
Warm-up: Review *Repaso,* p. 419 *A escribir,* p. 418 Review for the test on *Lección 18*	Video Program, Episode 9 Select an activity from *Capítulo 9* to include in the *Somos así* Portfolio Assessment. Suggestion: Checklist appropriate items on appendices C, D, E, F, G, H, I and J, as needed.

Notes

 Day 20

Textbook	Support Materials
Test on *Lección 18*	Student Test Booklet, Activities 1-12, pp. 151-158 Test Booklet Teacher's Edition, pp. 52-54 Audiocassette/Audio CD listening comprehension test (Side A, tracks 6-10) Oral Proficiency Evaluation Manual, Activities 1-3, pp. 56-58 Select an activity from *Capítulo 9* to include in the *Somos así* Portfolio Assessment. Suggestion: Checklist appropriate items on appendices C, D, E, F, G, H, I and J, as needed.

Notes

Capítulo 10, lecciones 19 y 20

Day 1

Textbook	Support Materials
Warm-up: Review *El subjuntivo: un resumen,* p. 398-399	AC/CD: *Un amigo por e-mail* (Side A, track 1)
Review the test on *Lección 18*	Quiz/Listening Activity 1, pp. L83-L84 (Side B, track 29)
Chapter preview: Discuss the chapter opener, pp. 420-421	Transparency 63
Un amigo por e-mail, p. 422	Workbook Activity 1, p. 191
Activities 1-3, pp. 422-423	AC/CD: Activities 1-2 (Side A, tracks 2-3)
Conexión cultural, p. 423	Quiz/Listening Activity 2, p. L85 (Side B, track 30)
	Workbook Activity 2, p. 192
	Quiz/Written Activity 1, p. W119

Notes

Day 2

Textbook	Support Materials
Warm-up: Review *Un amigo por e-mail,* p. 422	Workbook Activities 3-5, pp. 193-194
Activities 4-5, p. 424	Quiz/Written Activity 2, p. W120
Oportunidades, p. 424	AC/CD: Activity 7 (Side A, track 4)
Activity 6, p. 425	Quiz/Listening Activity 3, p. L86 (Side B, track 31)
Repaso rápido, p. 425	
Para ti: Proverbios y dichos, p. 426	
Activities 7-10, pp. 426-427	

Notes

Day 3

Textbook	Support Materials
Warm-up: Review *El pretérito perfecto y el participio*, p. 425 *Estrategia*, p. 427 Activities 11-12, pp. 428-429 *Autoevaluación*, p. 429 *¡La práctica hace al maestro!*, Activities A-B, p. 430 Review for the test on *Lección 19*	Workbook Activities 6-8, pp. 195-196 Quizzes/Written Activities 3-4, pp. W121-W122 Oral Proficiency Evaluation Manual, Activities 1-3, pp.59-61 Select an activity from *Capítulo 10* to include in the *Somos así* Portfolio Assessment. Suggestion: Activity 12, p. 428, Appendices B-1 and F-1

Notes

Day 4

Textbook	Support Materials
Test on *Lección 19*	Student Test Booklet, Activities 1-11, pp. 159-164 Test Booklet Teacher's Edition, pp. 54-56 Audiocassette/Audio CD listening comprehension test (Side A, tracks 11-14) Oral Proficiency Evaluation Manual, Activities 1-3, pp.59-61 Select an activity from *Capítulo 10* to include in the *Somos así* Portfolio Assessment. Suggestion: Activity 12, p. 428, Appendices B-1 and F-1

Notes

Day 5	**Textbook**	**Support Materials**

Warm-up: Review having students tell about an interesting recent email
Review the test on *Lección 19*
Un nuevo mundo, p. 432
Activities 1-2, p. 433
Para ti: Quisiera, p. 433
Conexión cultural, p. 433

AC/CD: *Un nuevo mundo* (Side B, track 5)
Quiz/Listening Activity 1, p. L87 (Side B, track 32)
Transparency 64
Workbook Activity 1, p. 197
AC/CD: Activities 1-2 (Side B, tracks 6-7)
Quiz/Listening Activity 2, p. L87 (Side B, track 33)
Workbook Activity 2, p. 198
Quiz/Written Activity 1, p. W123

Notes

Day 6	**Textbook**	**Support Materials**

Warm-up: Review *Un nuevo mundo,* p. 432
Activities 3-5, p. 434
Oportunidades, p. 435
Activities 6-7, pp. 435-436
Oportunidades, p. 436
Activities 8-9, p. 437

Workbook Activities 3-4, pp. 198-199
Quiz/Written Activity 2, p. W124
Workbook Activities 5-6, pp. 200-203
Video Program, Episode 10

Notes

Day 7 | **Textbook** | **Support Materials**

Warm-up: Review having students tell about
 their post-high school plans
Activities 10-11, p. 438
Para ti: ¡Ojo!, p. 438
Activities 12-13, p. 439
Autoevaluación, p. 439
¡La práctica hace al maestro!, Activities A-B,
 p. 440

Quiz/Listening Activity 3, p. L88 (Side B,
 track 34)
Quiz/Written Activity 3, p. W125
Workbook, Activity 7, p. 204
Quizzes/Written Activities 4-5, p.126

Notes

Day 8 | **Textbook** | **Support Materials**

Warm-up: Review *Repaso,* p. 447
A leer, Activities A-B, pp. 442-445
A escribir, p. 446
Review for the test on *Lección 20*

AC/CD: *Oportunidades para el futuro*
 (Side B, track 8)
AC/CD: Activities A-B (Side B, tracks 9-10)
Oral Proficiency Evaluation Manual,
 Activities 1-3, pp. 62-64
Select an activity from *Capítulo 10* to
 include in the *Somos así* Portfolio
 Assessment.
 Suggestion: Checklist appropriate items
 on appendices C, D, E, F, G, H, I and J,
 as needed.

Notes

Day 9

Textbook	Support Materials
Test on *Lección 20*	Student Test Booklet, Activities 1-11, pp. 165-170 Test Booklet Teacher's Edition, pp. 57-59 Audiocassette/Audio CD listening comprehension test (Side A, tracks 15-18) Oral Proficiency Evaluation Manual, Activities 1-3, pp. 62-64 Select an activity from *Capítulo 10* to include in the *Somos así* Portfolio Assessment. Suggestion: Checklist appropriate items on appendices C, D, E, F, G, H, I and J, as needed.

Notes

Day 10

Textbook	Support Materials
Achievement Test II	Student Test Booklet, Activities 1-24, pp. 171-184 Test Booklet Teacher's Edition, pp. 59-64 Audiocassette/Audio CD listening comprehension test (Side B, tracks 19-28) Oral Proficiency Evaluation Manual, Activities 1-5, pp. 65-68 Select an activity from *Capítulos 6-10* to include in the *Somos así* Portfolio Assessment. Suggestion: Checklist appropriate items on appendices C, D, E, F, G, H, I and J, as needed.

Notes

BLOCK SCHEDULE (90 MINUTES)

Capítulo 1, lecciones 1 y 2

 Day 1

Textbook	Support Materials
Chapter preview: Discuss chapter opener, pp. xxii and 1	AC/CD: *Conectados con el mundo* (Side A, track 1)
Conectados con el mundo, pp. 2-3	AC/CD: Activity 1 (Side A, track 2)
Activity 1, p. 3	Transparency 1
Algo más, p. 4	AC/CD: Activity 2 (Side A, track 3)
Para ti: ¿Inglés o español?, p. 4	Workbook Activity 1, p. 1
Activity 2, p. 4	Quiz/Written, Activity 1, p. W1
Conexión cultural, p. 4	Workbook Activity 2, p. 2
Activity 3, p. 4	Transparency 2
Repaso rápido, p. 5	Quiz/Listening Activity 1, p. L1 (Side A, track 1)
Para ti: En los Apéndices, p. 5	
Activities 4-9, pp. 5-7	Transparencies 3-4
Para ti: Más para hablar del tiempo, p. 7	Workbook Activities 3-4, pp. 3-4
Activities 10–11, p. 7	AC/CD: Activity 12 (Side A, track 4)
Repaso rápido, p. 8	Quiz/Listening Activity 2, p. L2 (Side A, track 2)
Activity 12, p. 8	
Idioma, p. 9	Workbook Activities 5-6, pp. 5-6
Activities 13-14, pp. 9-10	AC/CD: Activity 13 (Side A, track 5)
La mejor compañera, p. 10	Workbook Activity 7, p. 7
Activities 15-16, pp. 10-11	Quiz/Written Activity 2, p. W2
Para ti: Proverbios y dichos, p. 11	AC/CD: *La mejor compañera* (Side A, track 7)
Conexión cultural, p. 11	AC/CD: Activities 14-16 (Side A, tracks 6, 8 and 9)
Activity 17, p. 12	
Oportunidades, p. 12	Workbook Activity 8, p. 8
Repaso rápido, p. 12	Quiz/Listening Activity 3, p. L3 (Side A, track 3)
Activities 18-19, p. 13	
Para ti: ir a, p. 13	Workbook Activities 9-10, pp. 8-9
Activity 20, p. 13	Quiz/Written Activity 3, p. W3
	Transparency 5

Notes

Day 2 | **Textbook** | **Support Materials**

Textbook	Support Materials
Warm-up: Review stem-changing verbs, pp. 9 and 12	Workbook Activities 11-12, pp. 10-11
Idioma, p. 14	Quiz/Listening Activity 4, p. L4
Activities 21-22, p. 15	Workbook Activity 13, p. 12
Algo más, p. 15	Quiz/Written Activity 4, p. W4
Activities 23-25, pp. 16-17	Student Test Booklet, Activities 1-14, pp. 1-8
Autoevaluación, p. 17	Test Booklet Teacher's Edition, pp. 1-3
¡*La práctica hace al maestro!*, Activities A-B, p. 18	Audiocassette/Audio CD listening comprehension test (Side A, tracks 1-5)
Review for the test on *Lección 1*	Oral Proficiency Evaluation Manual, Activities 1-3, pp. 1-3
Test on *Lección 1*	Select an activity from *Capítulo 1* to include in the *Somos así* Portfolio Assessment. Suggestion: Activity A, p. 18, Appendices B and F

Notes

Day 3	**Textbook**	**Support Materials**

Warm-up: Review *Vocabulario*, p. 19
Review the test on *Lección 1*
¿Qué hiciste el pasado mes de junio?, p. 20
Activities 1-2, p. 21
Para ti: Acabar de, p. 21
Conexión cultural, p. 21
Activity 3, p. 22
Oportunidades, p. 22
Repaso rápido, pp. 22-23
Activities 4-8, pp. 23-25
Después de clases, p. 25
Activities 9-10, p. 26
Para ti: Más quehaceres en la casa, p. 26
Algo más, p. 26
Repaso rápido, p. 27
Activities 11-15, pp. 27-29
Idioma, p. 30
Activities 16-19, pp. 30-31
Algo más, p. 32
Activities 20-22, pp. 32-33

AC/CD: *Escuela virtual* (Side B, track 10)
Transparencies 6-7
AC/CD: Activities 1-2 (Side B, tracks 11-12)
Workbook Activity 1, p. 13
Quiz/Listening Activity 1, p. L5 (Side A, track 5)
Workbook Activities 2-5, pp. 14-17
Quiz/Written Activity 1, W5
AC/CD: Activity 4 (Side B, track 13)
AC/CD: *Después de clases* (Side B, tracks 14-15)
Transparencies 8-9
AC/CD: Activities 9-10 (Side B, tracks 16-17)
Quiz/Listening Activity 2, p. L6 (Side A, track 6)
Workbook Activities 6-8, pp. 18-20
Quiz/Written Activity 2, p. W6
Transparency 10
Workbook Activity 9, p. 21
Quiz/Written Activity 3, p. W7
AC/CD: Activity 19 (Side B, track 18)
Quiz/Listening Activity 3, p. L7 (Side A, track 7)
Workbook Activities 10-11, pp. 22-23
Quiz/Written Activity 4, p. W8

Notes

Textbook	Support Materials
Warm-up: Review double object pronoun use, p. 30	Workbook Activity 12, p. 24
Autoevaluación, p. 33	AC/CD: *En la Internet* (Side B, track 19)
¡La práctica hace al maestro!, Activities A-B, p. 34	AC/CD: Activities A-B (Side B, tracks 20-21)
A leer, Activities A-B, pp. 36-37	Video Program, Episode 1
A escribir, p. 38	Student Test Booklet, Activities 1-16, pp. 9-16
Review for the test on *Lección 2*	Test Booklet Teacher's Edition, pp. 3-6
Test on *Lección 2*	Audiocassette/Audio CD listening comprehension test (Side A, tracks 6-11)
	Oral Proficiency Evaluation Manual, Activities 1-3, pp. 4-6
	Select an activity from *Capítulo 1* to include in the *Somos así* Portfolio Assessment. Suggestion: Checklist appropriate items on appendices F, G, H, I and J, as needed.

Notes

Capítulo 2, lecciones 3 y 4

Day 1	Textbook	Support Materials
	Warm-up: *Repaso*, p. 39	AC/CD: *Somos muy diferentes.* (Side A, tracks 1-2)
	Review the test on *Lección 2*	Workbook Activity 1, p. 25
	Chapter preview: Discuss chapter opener, pp. 40-41	AC/CD Activities 1-2 (Side A, tracks 3-4)
	Somos muy diferentes, p. 42	Quiz/Written Activity 1, p. W9
	Activity 1, p. 43	AC/CD: *Lugares en los Estados Unidos con nombres en español* (Side A, track 5)
	Para ti: Hablando del pelo, p. 43	
	Activities 2-3, p. 43	Transparency 11
	Conexión cultural, p. 44	Workbook Activity 2, p. 26
	Activity 4, p. 44	Quiz/Written Activity 2, p. W10
	Oportunidades, p. 45	Quiz/Listening Activity 1, p. L9 (Side A, track 8)
	Activity 5, p. 45	
	Idioma, pp. 45-46	Workbook Activities 3-4, pp. 27-28
	Activity 6, p. 46	Quiz/Listening Activity 2, p. L9 (Side A, track 9)

Notes

Textbook	Support Materials
Warm-up: Review *los verbos reflexivos*, p. 45	Transparency 12
Algo más, p. 46	Workbook Activity 5, p. 29
Activities 7-11, pp. 47-48	Quiz/Written Activity 3, p. W11
Estrategia, p. 49	AC/CD: Activities 9-11 (Side A, tracks 6-8)
Para ti: Proverbios y dichos, p. 49	Quiz/Written Activity 4, p. W12
Activities 12-13, pp. 49-50	Quiz/Listening Activity 3, p. L10 (Side A, track 10)
Algo más p. 50	
Activities 14-17, pp. 50-51	Workbook Activity 6, p. 29
Algo más, p. 52	Quiz/Written Activity 5, p. W13
Activities 18-19, pp. 52-53	AC/CD: Activity 20 (Side A, track 9)
Idioma, p. 53	Quiz/Listening Activity 4, p. L10 (Side A, track 11)
Activity 20, p. 53	
	Workbook Activities 7-8, p. 30

Notes

Textbook	Support Materials
Warm-up: Review *el pretérito de los verbos reflexivos*, p. 52	Quiz/Listening Activity 5, p. L11 (Side A, track 12)
Conexión cultural, p. 54	Quiz/Written Activity 6, p. W14
Activities 21-22, p. 55	AC/CD: *Una toalla, por favor* (Side A, track 10)
Una toalla, por favor, p. 55	
Para ti: Otras palabras y expresiones, p. 56	Quiz/Listening Activity 6, p. L12 (Side A, track 13)
Activities 23-25, p. 56	Transparencies 13-14
Repaso rápido, p. 57	Workbook Activities 9-10, pp. 31-32
Idioma, p. *57*	AC/CD: Activity 24 (Side A, track 11)
Activities 26-28, pp. 58-59	Quiz/Listening Activity 7, p. L12 (Side A, track 14)
	Workbook Activity 11, p. 33
	Quiz/Written Activity 7, p. W14

Notes

Day 4

Textbook	Support Materials
Warm-up: Review *los adjetivos y pronombres demostrativos*, p. 57	Workbook Activity 12, p. 34
¡La práctica hace al maestro!, Activities A-B, p. 60	Student Test Booklet, Activities 1-13, pp. 17-24
Practice *Vocabulario,* p. 61	Test Booklet Teacher's Edition, pp. 6-9
Autoevaluación, p. 59	Audiocassette/Audio CD listening comprehension test (Side A, tracks 12-15)
Review for the test on *Lección 3*	Oral Proficiency Evaluation Manual, Activities 1-3, pp. 7-9
Test on *Lección 3*	Select an activity from *Capítulo 2* to include in the *Somos así* Portfolio Assessment. Suggestion: Activity 18, p. 52, Appendices B and F

Notes

Day 5	Textbook	Support Materials
	Warm-up: Review reflexive verbs.	AC/CD: *No me siento bien* (Side B, track 13)
	Review the test on *Lección 3*	
	No me siento bien, p. 62	AC/CD: Activity 1 (Side B, track 14)
	Para ti: La palabra pescar, p. 62	Workbook Activity 1, p. 35
	Activities 1-2, pp. 62-63	AC/CD: Activity 2 (Side B, track 15)
	Conexión cultural, p. 63	AC/CD: *Aquí se habla español* (Side B, track 16)
	Activity 3, p. 64	
	Oportunidades, p. 64	Workbook Activity 2, p. 36
	Activity 4, p. 64	Quizzes/Written Activities 1-2, pp. W15-W16
	El cuerpo, p. 65	
	Activity 5, p. 65	AC/CD: *El cuerpo* (Side B, track 17)
	Para ti: Más palabras del cuerpo, p. 65	Quiz/Listening Activity 1, p. L13 (Side 15, track 15)
	Activities 6-8, p. 66	
	Algo más, p. 67	Transparencies 15-16
	Activities 9-10, p. 67	Workbook Activities 3-4, pp. 36-37
		AC/CD: Activity 8 (Side B, track 18)
		Quiz/Listening Activity 2, p. L14 (Side A, track 16)
		Workbook Activity 5, p. 38
		Quiz/Written Activity 3, p. W17

Notes

Day 6	Textbook	Support Materials

Textbook	Support Materials
Warm-up: Review *¿Qué oyes en el consultorio del médico?*, p. 67	AC/CD: Activity 11 (Side B, track 19)
Activity 11, p. 68	Workbook Activity 6, p. 39
Idioma, p. 68	Quiz/Written Activity 4, p. W18
Activities 12-14, pp. 68-69	AC/CD: Activity 14 (Side B, track 20)
Algo más, p. 69	Workbook Activity 7, p. 40
Activities 15-17, pp. 70-71	Quiz/Written Activity 5, p. W18
En el médico, p. 71	AC/CD: *En el médico* (Side B, tracks 21-22)
Activity 18, p. 72	Quiz/Listening Activity 3, p. L14 (Side A, track 17)
Para ti: ¿Doctor?, p. 72	AC/CD: Activities 18-19 (Side B, tracks 23-24)
Activities 19-20, p. 72	Quiz/Listening Activity 4, p. L15 (Side A, track 18)
Algo más, p. 73	Workbook Activities 8-9, pp. 40-42
Activity 21, p. 73	

Notes

Textbook	**Support Materials**
Warm-up: Review *Verbos similares*, p. 73	Quizzes/Listening Activities 5-6,
Activity 22, p. 74	pp. L15-L16 (Side A, tracks 19-20)
Repaso rápido, p. 74	Workbook Activity 10, p. 43
Idioma, p. 74	Quiz/Written Activity 6, p. W19
Activities 23-25, p. 75	AC/CD: Activities 23-24 (Side B, tracks
Autoevaluación, p. 75	25-26)
¡La práctica hace al maestro!, Activities A-B,	Workbook Activity 11, p. 44
p. 76	Video Program, Episode 2
Review *Vocabulario*, p. 77	

Notes

Warm-up: Review reflexive verbs
A leer, Activities A-B, pp. 78-79
A escribir, p. 80
Review for the test on *Lección 4*
Test on *Lección 4*

AC/CD: *La vida de una atleta profesional* (Side B, track 27)
AC/CD: Activities A-B (Side B, tracks 28-29)
Quiz/Listening Activity 7, p. L16 (Side A, track 21)
Quiz/Written Activity 7, p. W20
Student Test Booklet, Activities 1-12, pp. 25-32
Test Booklet Teacher's Edition, pp. 9-11
Audiocassette/Audio CD listening comprehension test (Side A, tracks 16-19)
Oral Proficiency Evaluation Manual, Activities, Activities 1-3, pp. 10-12
Select an activity from *Capítulo 2* to include in the *Somos así* Portfolio Assessment. Suggestion: Checklist appropriate items on appendices F, G, H, I and J, as needed.

Notes

Capítulo 3, lecciones 5 y 6

Day 1	Textbook	Support Materials
	Warm-up: Review everyday activities, commands (used in a doctor's office), foods	AC/CD: *En la ciudad* (Side A, tracks 1-2)
		Quiz/Listening Activity 1, P. L17 (Side B, track 22)
	Review the test on *Lección 4*	Transparencies 17-18
	Chapter preview: Discuss chapter opener, pp. 82-83	Workbook Activity 1, p. 45
	En la ciudad, p. 84	AC/CD: Activities 1-2 (Side A, tracks 3-4)
	Activities 1-2, p. 85	Quiz/Written Activity 1, pp. W21-W22
	Conexión cultural, p. 86	AC/CD: *México* (Side A, track 5)
	Activity 3, p. 87	Quiz/Listening Activity 2, p. L18 (Side B, track 23)
	Estrategia, p. 87	Workbook Activity 2, p. 46
	Algo más, p. 87	AC/CD: Activity 3 (Side A, track 6)
	Para ti: Más tiendas en la ciudad, p. 87	Quiz/Listening Activity 3, p. L18 (Side B, track 24)
	Activities 4-6, pp. 88-89	Transparency 19
	Idioma, p. 89	Workbook Activity 3, p. 46
	Para ti: Proverbios y dichos, p. 90	Quiz/Written Activity 2, p. W23
	Activities 7-12, pp. 90-92	AC/CD: Activities 4-6 (Side A, tracks 7-9)
		Quiz/Listening Activity 4, p. L19 (Side B, track 25)
		Workbook Activities 4-6, pp. 47-49
		Quizzes/Written Activities 3-4, pp. W25-W26
		AC/CD: *En la ciudad* (Side A, tracks 1-2)

Notes

Day 2	Textbook	Support Materials

Warm-up: Review, talk with students about Mexican-American foods they have eaten

¿Qué le gustaría ordenar?, p. 93

Activity 13, p. 93

Para ti: Más palabras, p. 93

Conexión cultural, pp. 94-95

Activities 14-15, p. 96

Oportunidades, p. 96

Idioma, p. 97

Activities 16-19, pp. 98-99

Algo más, p. 100

Activities 20-22, pp. 100-101

AC/CD: *¿Qué le gustaría ordenar?* (Side B, track 10)

AC/CD: Activity 13 (Side B, track 11)

Workbook Activity 7, p. 50

Quiz/Written Activity 5, pp. W26-W27

AC/CD: Activity 14 (Side B, track 12)

AC/CD: *¿Qué le gustaría ordenar?* (Side B, track 10)

Quizzes/Listening Activities 5-6, pp. L19-L20 (Side B, tracks 26-27)

Workbook Activities 8-9, p. 51

Quiz/Written 6, p. W27

AC/CD: Activities 19-21 (Side B, tracks 13-15)

Workbook Activity 10, p. 52

Notes

Day 3	Textbook	Support Materials

Textbook

Warm-up: Review affirmative and formal commands, pp. 89 and 97

Idioma, p. 101

Activities 23-25, pp. 102-103

Autoevaluación, p. 103

¡La práctica hace al maestro!, Activity A, p. 104

Support Materials

Quiz/Listening Activity 7, p. L20 (Side B, track 28)

Workbook Activity 11, p. 53

Quiz/Written Activity 7, p. W28

AC/CD: Activity 23 (Side B, track 16)

Workbook Activity 12, p. 54

Notes

Warm-up: Review for the test on *Lección 5*
¡La práctica hace al maestro!, Activity B,
   p. 104
Test on *Lección 5*

Student Test Booklet, Activities 1-13,
   pp. 33-40
Test Booklet Teacher's Edition, pp. 11-14
Audiocassette/Audio CD listening
   comprehension test (Side B, tracks 20-23)
Oral Proficiency Evaluation Manual,
   Activities 1-3, pp. 13-15
Select an activity from *Capítulo 3* to include
   in the *Somos así* Portfolio Assessment.
   Suggestion: Activity A, p. 104,
   Appendices B and F

Notes

Textbook

Warm-up: Review places in the city, affirmative commands
Review the test on *Lección 5*
En el barrio Las Lomas, p. 106
Activity 1, p. 106
Algo más, p. 107
Activity 2, p. 107
Oportunidades, p. 107
Conexión cultural, p. 108
Activity 3, p. 109
Idioma, p. 110
Activities 4-9, pp. 111-112
Algo más, p. 113
Activities 10-11, pp. 113-114

Support Materials

AC/CD: *En el barrio Las Lomas* (Side A, tracks 1-2)
AC/CD: Activity 1 (Side A, track 3)
Quiz/Listening Activity 1, p. L21 (Side B, track 29)
Workbook Activity 1, p. 55
AC/CD: Activity 2 (Side A, track 4)
Quiz/Listening Activity 2, p. L22 (Side B, track 30)
Workbook Activity 2, p. 56
AC/CD: *México hoy* (Side A. track 5)
Quiz/Listening Activity 3, p. L22 (Side B, track 31)
Workbook Activities 3-5, pp. 57-58
Quiz/Written Activity 1, p. W29
AC/CD: Activities 5, 6 and 9 (Side A, tracks 6-8)
Workbook Activity 6, p. 59
Quiz/Written Activity 2, p. W30
AC/CD: Activity 11 (Side A, track 9)

Notes

Day 6

Textbook	Support Materials
Warm-up: Review the formation of affirmative commands	AC/CD: *En casa de Pablo* (Side B, track 10)
En casa de Pablo, p. 115	AC/CD: Activities 12-13 (Side B, tracks 11-12)
Activities 12-13, p. 115	Quiz/Listening Activity 4, p. L 23 (Side B, track 32)
Idioma, p. 116	Workbook Activities 7-8, pp. 59-60
Activities 14-20, pp. 116-119	Quizzes/Written Activities 3-4, pp. W31-W32
Algo más, p. 119	AC/CD: Activities 15-16 (Side B, tracks 13-14)
Activities 21-24, pp. 120-121	Quiz/Listening Activity 5, p. L23 (Side B, track 33)
¡Qué coches!, p. 122	Workbook Activity 9, p. 61
Para ti: Más palabras para el coche, p. 122	Quiz/Written Activity 5, p. W33
Activities 25-27, pp. 122-123	AC/CD: Activity 21 (Side B, track 15)
	AC/CD: *¡Qué coches!* (Side B, tracks 16-17)
	AC/CD: Activity 25 (Side B, track 18)
	Transparencies 20-21
	Workbook Activities 10-11, pp.62-63
	Quiz/Written Activity 6, p. W34-W35
	AC/CD: Activity 27 (Side B, track 19)

Notes

Day 7

Textbook	Support Materials
Warm-up: Review vocabulary associated with getting around in a city *Las señales de tráfico,* p. 124 Activity 28, p. 124 *¡La práctica hace al maestro!,* Activities A-B, p. 126 *¡Conozca México!,* p. 128 *A leer,* Activities A-B, p. 128-129	AC/CD: *Las señales de tráfico* (Side B, track 20) Quiz/Listening Activity 6, p. L 24 (Side B, track 34) Transparencies 22-25 Workbook Activities 12, p. 64 AC/CD: *¡Conozca México!* (Side B, track 21) Quiz/Written Activity 7, p. W36 AC/CD: Activities A-B (Side B, tracks 22-23) Video Program, Episode 3

Notes

Textbook	Support Materials
Warm-up: Review what students have learned about Mexico *Autoevaluación*, p. 125 Review for the test on *Lección 6* *A escribir*, p. 130 Test on *Lección 6*	Student Test Booklet, Activities 1-15, pp. 41-48 Test Booklet Teacher's Edition, pp. 14-17 Audiocassette/Audio CD listening comprehension test (Side B, tracks 24-28) Oral Proficiency Evaluation Manual, Activities 1-3, pp. 16-18 Select an activity from *Capítulo 3* to include in the *Somos así* Portfolio Assessment. Suggestion: Checklist items on appendices C, D, E, F, G, H, I and J, as needed.

Notes

Capítulo 4, lecciones 7 y 8

Day 1

Textbook	Support Materials
Warm-up: Review *Partes del coche*, p. 127	AC/CD: *Un día en el parque de atracciones* (Side A, tracks 1-2)
Review the test on *Lección 6*	
Chapter preview: Discuss chapter opener, pp. 132-133	Quiz/Listening Activity 1, p. L25 (Side A, track 1)
Un día en el parque de atracciones, pp. 134-135	Transparencies 26-27
Activities 1-3, p. 135	Workbook Activity 1, p. 65
Conexión cultural, p. 136	AC/CD: Activities 1-2 (Side A, tracks 3-4)
Activity 4, p. 137	AC/CD: *El Salvador* (Side A, track 5)
Oportunidades, p. 137	Quiz/Listening Activity 2, p. L25 (Side A, track 2,)
Idioma, pp. 137-138	Workbook Activity 2, p. 66
Activities 5-8, pp. 139-140	Quiz/Listening Activity 3, p. L26 (Side A, track 3)
Algo más, p. 140	Workbook Activities 3-4, pp. 67-68
Activities 9-10, p. 141	Quiz/Written Activity 1, p. W37
	AC/CD: Activities 5-6 (Side A, tracks 6-7)
	Workbook Activities 5-6, p. 69
	Quiz/Written Activity 2, p. W38
	AC/CD: Activity 9 (Side A, track 8)

Notes

Textbook	**Support Materials**
Warm-up: Review *Los usos del imperfecto*, p. 140	AC/CD: Activity 11 (Side A, track 9)
Activities 11-12, p. 142	AC/CD: *Una visita al jardín zoológico* (Side B, tracks 10-11)
Una visita al jardín zoológico, p. 143	Quiz/Listening Activity 4, p. L27 (Side A, track 40
Activity 13, p. 144	Transparencies 28-29
Algo más, p. 144	Workbook Activities 7-8, p. 70
Activity 14, p. 144	Quiz/Written Activity 3, p. W39
Algo más, p. 145	AC/CD: Activities 13-14 (Side B, tracks 12-13)
Para ti: Más animales, p. 145	Quiz/Written Activity 4, p. W40
Activities 15-16, pp. 145-146	Quizzes/Listening Activities 5-6, pp. L127-L128 (Side A, tracks 5-6)
Idioma, p. 146	Workbook Activities 9-11, pp. 71-72
Algo más, p. 146	Quizzes/Written Activities 5-6, pp. W40-W41
Activities 17-18, p. 147	AC/CD: Activity 18 (Side B, track 14)
Para ti: Los monos, p. 147	Transparency 30
Activity 19, p. 148	

Notes

Textbook	Support Materials
Warm-up: Review *Más sobre los usos del imperfecto*, p. 146	AC/CD: Activity 20 and 22 (Side B, tracks 15-16)
Activities 20-21, p. 149	Workbook Activity 12, p. 73
Estrategia, p. 150	Quiz/Listening Activity 7, p. L28 (Side A, track 7)
Activities 22-23, pp. 150-151	
Algo más, p. 151	Workbook Activity 13, pp. 74-75
Activities 24-26, pp. 152-153	Quiz/Written Activity 7, p. W42
Repaso rápido, p. 153	AC/CD: Activity 28 (Side B, track 17)
Activities 27-28, pp. 154-155	Oral Proficiency Evaluation Manual, Activities 1-3, pp. 19-21

Notes

Day 4	Textbook	Support Materials

Warm up: Review the uses of *ser* vs. *estar*,
  p. 153
Autoevaluación, p. 155
¡La práctica hace al maestro!, Activities A-B,
  p. 156
Review *Vocabulario,* p. 157
Review for the test on *Lección 7*
Test on *Lección 7*

Workbook Activity 14, p. 76
Student Test Booklet, Activities 1-13,
  pp. 49-56
Test Booklet Teacher's Edition, pp. 17-19
Audiocassette/Audio CD listening
  comprehension test (Side A, tracks 1-4)
Oral Proficiency Evaluation Manual,
  Activities 1-3, pp. 19-21
Select an activity from *Capítulo 4* to include
  in the *Somos así* Portfolio Assessment.
  Suggestion: Activity 27, p. 154,
  Appendices B and F

Notes

Day 5	Textbook	Support Materials

Textbook

Warm-up: Review nationalities and animal
   vocabulary
Review the test on *Lección 7*
El Gran Circo de las Estrellas, p. 158
Activities 1-3, p. 159
Conexión cultural, p. 160
Activity 4, p. 161
Idioma, p. 161
Activities 5-7, p. 162
Repaso rápido, p. 163
Activities 8-9, p. 164
Idioma, pp. 165-166
Activity 10, p. 166

Support Materials

AC/CD: *El Gran Circo de las Estrellas*
   (Side A, tracks 1-2)
Quiz/Listening Activity 1, p. L 29 (Side A,
   track 8)
Transparencies 31-32
Workbook Activity 1, p. 77
AC/CD: Activities 1-2 (Side A, tracks 3-4)
AC/CD: *Honduras* (Side A, track 5)
Quiz/Listening Activity 2, p. L30 (Side A,
   track 9)
Workbook Activities 2-4, pp. 78-79
Quizzes/Written Activities 1-2,
   pp. W43-W44
AC/CD: Activity 9 (Side A, track 6)
Quiz/Listening Activity 3, p. L30 (Side A,
   track 10)
Workbook Activities 5-6, pp. 80-81
Quiz/Written Activity 3, p. W45

Notes

Textbook	Support Materials
Warm-up: Review *Los adjetivos y su posición*, p. 165	Transparency 33
Activities 11-12, p. 167	AC/CD: *¿Qué pasó en la finca?* (Side B, tracks 7-8)
Para ti: Los adjetivos como sustantivos, p. 167	Quiz/Listening Activity 4, p. L31 (Side A, track 11)
Activity 13, p. 168	
¿Qué pasó en la finca?, pp. 168-169	Transparencies 34-35
Activities 14-18, pp. 169-170	Workbook Activity 7, p. 82
Lo que los animales dicen, p. 170	Quiz/Written Activity 4, p. W46
Algo más, p. 170	AC/CD: Activities 14, 15 and 17 (Side B, tracks 9-11)
Activity 19, p. 171	
Para ti: Proverbios y dichos, p. 171	AC/CD: *Lo que los animales dicen* (Side B, track 12)
Activity 20, p. 171	
Idioma, p. 172	Quiz/Listening Activity 5, p. L31 (Side A, track 12)
Algo más, p. 170	
Activities 21-24, pp. 173-174	Workbook Activities 8-9, p. 83
Algo más, p. 174	Quiz/Written Activity 5, p. W46
Activities 25-26, pp. 174-175	AC/CD: Activity 21 (Side B, track 13)
	Workbook Activity 10, p. 84
	Quiz/Written Activity 6, p. W47
	AC/CD: Activity 26 (Side B, track 14)

Notes

Day 7	Textbook	Support Materials

Warm-up: Review *Los adjetivos y pronombres posesivos*, pp. 172 and 174
Algo más, p. 175
Activity 27, p. 176
Algo más, p. 176
Activity 28, pp. 176-177
Autoevaluación, p. 177
¡La práctica hace al maestro!, Activities A-B, p. 178
Review *Vocabulario*, p. 179
A leer, Activities A-B, pp. 180-181

Workbook Activity 11, p. 85
AC/CD: Activity 27 (Side B, track 15)
Quiz/Listening Activity 6, p. L32 (Side A, track 13)
Workbook Activities 12-13, pp. 85-86
AC/CD: *¡El Gran Circo de los Hermanos Suárez!* (Side B, track 16)
AC/CD: Activities A-B (Side B, tracks 17-18)
Quiz/Listening Activity 7, p. L33 (Side A, track 14)
Quiz/Written Activity 7, p. W48

Notes

Textbook	Support Materials
Warm-up: Review circus and farm vocabulary, p. 179 *A escribir,* p. 182 Review for the test on *Lección* 8 Test on *Lección* 8	Video Program, Episode 4 Student Test Booklet, Activities 1-12, pp. 57-64 Test Booklet Teacher's Edition, pp. 20-22 Audiocassette/Audio CD listening comprehension test (Side A, tracks 5-8) Oral Proficiency Evaluation Manual, Activities 1-3, pp. 22-24 Select an activity from *Capítulo 4* to include in the *Somos así* Portfolio Assessment. Suggestion: Checklist appropriate items on appendices F, G, H, I and J, as needed.

Notes

Capítulo 5, lecciones 9 y 10

Day 1

Textbook	Support Materials
Warm-up: Review *los pronombres y adjetivos posesivos,* pp. 172 and 174	AC/CD: *¿Dónde estuvieron Uds. anoche?* (Side A, track 1)
Review the test on *Lección 8*	Quiz/Listening Activity 1, p. L35 (Side B, track 15)
Chapter preview: Discuss chapter opener, pp. 184-185	Transparency 36
¿Dónde estuvieron Uds. anoche?, p. 186	AC/CD: Activities 1-2 (Side A, tracks 2-3)
Activities 1-2, p. 187	AC/CD: *Cuba: El Caribe a todo sol* (Side A, track 4)
Conexión cultural, p. 188	Quiz/Listening Activity 2, p. L35 (Side B, track 16)
Activity 3, p. 189	Workbook Activity 1, p. 87
Repaso rápido, p. 189	Quiz/Listening Activity 3, p. L36 (Side B, track 17)
Activities 4-5, p. 190	Workbook Activities 2-4, pp. 88-89
Para ti: El pretérito de conocer, p. 190	Quiz/Written Activity 1, p. W49
Activity 6, p. 191	AC/CD: Activity 6 (Side A, track 5)
Idioma, p. 191	Quiz/Listening Activity 4, p. L36 (Side B, track 18)
Activities 7-11, pp. 192-193	Workbook Activities 5-6, pp. 90-91
Algo más, p. 193	Quiz/Written Activity 2, p. W50
Activity 12, p. 194	Quiz/Listening Activity 5, p. L37 (Side B, track 19)
	Workbook Activity 7, p. 92
	Quiz/Written Activity 3, p. W51

Notes

Textbook	Support Materials
Warm-up: Review *El pretérito y el imperfecto*, p. 191	AC/CD: *¿Qué compraron?* (Side B, tracks 6-7)
¿Qué compraron?, p. 194	Transparencies 37-38
Activities 13-15, p. 195	AC/CD: Activities 13,14 and 16 (Side B, tracks 8-10)
Para ti: Más comida en el supermercado, p. 195	Workbook Activities 8-9, pp. 92-93
Idioma, p. 196	Quiz/Written Activity 4, p. W52
Estrategia, p. 196	AC/CD: Activity 17 (Side B, track 11)
Activities 16-17, pp. 196-197	Quiz/Written Activity 5, p. W53
Para ti: Los grados centígrados, p. 197	AC/CD: Activity 18 (Side B, track 12)
Conexión cultural, p. 197	Quiz/Listening Activity 6, p. L37 (Side B, track 20)
Activity 18, p. 198	Workbook Activities 10-11, pp. 94-95
Idioma, p. 198	Quiz/Written Activity 6, p. W54
Activities 19-23, pp. 199-201	AC/CD: Activity 20 (Side B, track 13)

Notes

Day 3	Textbook	Support Materials

Textbook

Warm-up: Review the uses of the preterite vs. the imperfect
El menú, p. 201
Activities 24-25, p. 202
Para ti: Más palabras en el menú, p. 202
Oportunidades, p. 203
Activities 26-28, pp. 203-205
Autoevaluación, p. 205
¡La práctica hace al maestro!, Activities A-B, p. 206
Review for the test on *Lección 9*

Support Materials

Quiz/Listening Activity 7, p. L38 (Side B, track 21)
Transparency 39
Workbook Activities 12-13, pp. 95-96
Quiz/Written Activity 7, pp. W55-W56
Workbook Activity 14, p. 96
Oral Proficiency Evaluation Manual, Activities 1-3, pp. 25-27
Select and Activity from *Capítulo 5* to include in the *Somos así* Portfolio Assessment.
Suggestion: Activity 22, p. 200, Appendices B and F

Notes

Textbook	Support Materials
Test on *Lección 9*	Student Test Booklet, Activities 1-14, pp. 65-72
Warm-up: Review irregular preterite forms, p. 198	Test Booklet Teacher's Edition, pp. 22-25
Buscando un vestido, p. 208	Audiocassette/Audio CD listening comprehension test (Side A, tracks 9-12)
Activities 1-2, p. 208	AC/CD: *Buscando un vestido* (Side A, track 1)
Para ti: Expresiones adicionales, p. 208	
Conexión cultural, p. 209	AC/CD: Activities 1-2 (Side A, tracks 2-3)
Activity 3, p. 210	Quiz/Listening Activity 1, p. L39 (Side B, track 22)
	Transparency 40
	Workbook Activity 1, p. 97
	AC/CD: *El Caribe* (Side A, track 4)
	Quiz/Listening Activity 2, p. L39 (Side B, track 23)
	Workbook Activity 2, p. 97

Notes

Day 5

Textbook	Support Materials
Warm-up: Review the dialog *Buscando un vestido*, p.208	Quiz/Listening Activity 3, p. L40 (Side B, track 23)
Review the test on *Lección 9*	Workbook Activities 3-4, pp. 98-99
Oportunidades, p. 210	Quiz/Written Activity 1, p. W57
Idioma, p. 210	AC/CD: Activity 4 (Side A, track 5)
Activities 4-6, pp. 211-212	Workbook Activities 5-6, pp. 100-101
Algo más, p. 212	AC/CD: Activities 7-8 (Side A, tracks 6-7)
Activities 7-9, pp. 213-214	AC/CD: *Buscando un vestido (continuación)* (Side B, track 8)
Buscando un vestido (continuación), pp. 214-215	Quiz/Listening Activity 4, p. L41 (Side B, track 24)
Activities 10-11, p. 215	
Para ti: Más palabras en la joyería, p. 215	Workbook Activity 7, p. 102
Algo más, p. 215	AC/CD: Activities 10-11 (Side B, tracks 9-10)
Activities 12-13, p. 216	Quiz/Written Activity 2, p. W58
Idioma, p. 216	Workbook Activity 8, p. 103
Activities 14-16, pp. 217-218	Quiz/Written Activity 3, p. W59

Notes

Textbook	**Support Materials**
Warm-up: Review *Los adverbios terminados en –mente*, p. 216	AC/CD: *La cena elegante* (Side B, track 11)
La cena elegante, p. 218	Quiz/Written Activity 4, p. W59
Activities 17-18, p. 219	AC/CD: Activities 17-18 (Side B, tracks 12-13)
Repaso rápido, p. 219	Workbook Activity 9, p. 104
Activity 19, p. 220	Quiz/Written Activity 5, p. W60
La cena elegante (continuación), p. 220	AC/CD: *La cena elegante (continuación)* (Side B, track 14)
Activities 20-21, pp.220-221	Quiz/Listening Activity 5, p. L42 (Side B, track 25)
Para ti: Proverbios y dichos, p. 221	Transparencies 41-42
Idioma, p. 221	Workbook Activity 10, p. 104
Activities 22-24, pp. 222-223	AC/CD: Activity 21 (Side B, track 15)
Autoevaluación, p. 223	Quiz/Listening Activity 6, p. L43 (Side B, track 26)
	Workbook Activity 11, p. 105
	Quiz/Written Activity 6, p. W61
	AC/CD: Activity 24 (Side B, track 16)

Notes

Day 7	Textbook	Support Materials

Textbook

Warm-up: Review the present and the imperfect progressive tenses

¡La práctica hace al maestro!, Activities A-B, p. 224

A leer, Activities A-B, pp. 226-227

A escribir, p. 228

Review for the test on *Lección 10*

Support Materials

Workbook Activity 12, p. 106

AC/CD: *El Caribe* (Side B, track 17)

Quiz/Listening Activity 7, p. L44 (Side B, track 27)

Quiz/Written Activity 7, p. W62

Video program, Episode 5

Oral Proficiency Evaluation Manual, Activities 1-3, pp. 28-30

Select an activity from *Capítulo 5* to include in the *Somos así* Portfolio Assessment. Suggestion: Checklist appropriate items on appendices F, G, H, I and J, as needed.

Notes

Textbook	**Support Materials**
Test on *Lección 10* Achievement Test 1	Student Test Booklet, Activities 1-12, pp. 73-80 Test Booklet Teacher's Edition, pp. 25-28 Audiocassette/Audio CD listening comprehension test (Side A, tracks 13-16) Student Test Booklet, Activities 1-28, pp. 81-94 Test Booklet Teacher's Edition, pp. 28-33 Audiocassette/Audio CD listening comprehension test (Side B, tracks 17-27) Oral Proficiency Evaluation Manual, Activities 1-5, pp. 31-34 Select an activity from *Capítulos 1-5* to include in the *Somos así* Portfolio Assessment. Suggestion: Checklist appropriate items on appendices C, D, E, F, G, H, I and J, as needed.

Notes

Capítulo 6, lecciones 11 y 12

Day 1	Textbook	Support Materials
	Warm-up: Have students report about a past action or event	AC/CD: *En casa de Felipe* (Side A, track 1)
	Review the test on *Lección 10*	Transparency 43
	Review the Achievement Test 1	AC/CD: Activities 1-2 (Side A, tracks 2-3)
	Chapter preview: Discuss chapter opener, pp. 230-231	Quiz/Listening Activity 1, p. L45 (Side A, track 1)
	En casa de Felipe, p. 23	Quiz/Written Activity 2, p. W63
	Activities 1-3, p. 233	AC/CD: *Bolivia* (Side A, track 4)
	Para ti: Los quehaceres, p. 233	Quiz/Listening Activity 2, p. L46 (Side A, track 2)
	Conexión cultural, p. 234	Workbook Activity 1, p. 107
	Activity 4, p. 235	AC/CD: Activity 4 (Side A, track 5)
	Idioma, pp. 235-236	Quiz/Listening Activity 3, p. L46 (Side A, track 3)
	Activities 5-6, pp. 236-237	Quiz/Written Activity 2, p. W64
	Algo más, p. 237	Workbook Activity 2, p. 108
	Activities 7-9, pp. 238-239	Quiz/Written Activity 3, p. W65
		AC/CD: Activities 8-9 (Side A, tracks 6-7)

Notes

Day 2

Textbook	Support Materials
Warm-up: Review *El subjuntivo con mandatos indirectos*, p. 237	Workbook Activities 3-4, pp. 109-110
Idioma, p. 239	Quiz/Written Activity 4, p. W66
Activities 10-12, p. 240	AC/CD: *En la casa de Felipe (continuación)* (Side A, track 8)
En casa de Felipe (continuación), p. 241	AC/CD: Activity 13 (Side A, track 9)
Activity 13, p. 241	Quiz/Listening Activity 4, p. L47 (Side A, track 4)
Algo más, p. 242	
Activity 14, p. 242	Workbook Activity 5, p. 111
Para ti: Palabras de cariño, p. 242	Quiz/Listening Activity 5, p. L48
Idioma, p. 243	Workbook Activities 6-7, pp. 111-112
Activities 15-17, pp. 243-244	AC/CD: Activity 17 (Side A, track 10)
Trabajando en casa, p. 245	AC/CD: *Trabajando en casa* (Side B tracks 11-12)
Activity 18, p. 245	AC/CD: Activity 18 (Side B, track 13)
	Quiz/Listening Activity 6, p. L48 (Side A, track 5)
	Transparency 44
	Workbook Activity 8, p. 112

Notes

Textbook	Support Materials
Warm-up: Review dialog *Trabajando en casa,* p. 245	AC/CD: Activity 19 (Side B, track 14)
Activity 19, p. 246	Workbook Activity 9, p. 113
Algo más, p. 246	Quiz/Written Activity 5, p. W67
Activities 20-22, pp. 246-247	AC/CD: *Trabajando en casa (continuación)* (Side B, track 15)
Trabajando en casa (continuación), p. 248	AC/CD: Activity 23 (Side B, track 16)
Activity 23, p. 248	Workbook Activity 10, p. 114
Algo más, p. 248	Quiz/Written Activity 6, p. W67
Activities 24-25, p. 249	AC/CD: Activity 24 (Side B, track 17)
En la casa, p. 250	AC/CD: *En la casa* (Side B, track 18)
Activity 26, p. 250	Quiz/Listening Activity 7, p. L49 (Side A, track 7)
	Transparencies 45-46
	Workbook Activity 11, p. 115
	Quiz/Written Activity 7, p. W68

Notes

Textbook	Support Materials

Warm-up: Review vocabulary from *En la casa*, p. 250

Activities 27-28, p. 251

Para ti: La arquitectura hispana, p. 251

Autoevaluación, p. 251

¡La práctica hace al maestro!, Activities A-B, p. 252

Review for the test on *Lección 11*

Test on *Lección 11*

AC/CD: Activity 27 (Side B, track 19)

Transparency 47

Workbook Activity 12, p. 160

Student Test Booklet, Activities 1-13, pp. 95-102

Test Booklet Teacher's Edition, pp. 34-36

Audiocassette/Audio CD listening comprehension test (Side A, tracks 1-4)

Oral Proficiency Evaluation Manual, Activities 1-3, pp. 35-37

Select an activity from *Capítulo 6* to include in the *Somos así* Portfolio Assessment. Suggestion: Activity B, p. 252, Appendices B-1 and F-1

Notes

Textbook	Support Materials
Warm-up: Review house and family vocabulary and rules at home	AC/CD: *Las reglas de la casa* (Side A, tracks 1-2)
Review the test on *Lección 11*	Quiz/Listening Activity 1, p. L51 (Side A, track 8)
Las reglas de la casa, p. 254	AC/CD: Activities 1-2 (Side A, tracks 3-4)
Activities 1-2, p. 255	AC/CD: *Los países bolivianos* (Side A, track 5)
Estrategia, p. 255	Quiz/Listening Activity 2, p. L51 (Side A, track 9)
Conexión cultural, p. 256	Workbook Activities 1-3, pp. 117-119
Activity 3, p. 257	Quiz/Written Activity 1, p. W69
Idioma, p. 257	AC/CD: Activities 4 and 8 (Side A, tracks 6-7)
Activities 4-7, pp. 258-259	Workbook Activities 4-5, pp. 120-121
Algo más, p. 260	Quiz/Written Activity 2, p. W70
Activity 8, p. 260	

Notes

Textbook	Support Materials
Warm-up: Review *Otros verbos de emoción,* p. 260	Quiz/Listening Activity 3, p. L52 (Side A. track 10)
Activities 9-10, p. 261	Workbook Activities 6-7, pp. 122-123
Algo más, p. 262	Quiz/Written Activity 3, p. W71
Activities 11-12, p. 263	AC/CD: Activity 12 (Side A, track 8)
Para ti: Proverbios y dichos, p. 263	AC/CD: *La abuela cumple años* (Side B, track 9)
Activities 13-14, p. 264	Quiz/Listening Activity 4, p. L52 (Side A, track 11)
La abuela cumple años, p. 265	AC/CD: Activities 15-16 (Side B, tracks 10 and 12)
Activities 15-17, p. 266	AC/CD: *Algunos aparatos de la casa* (Side B, track 12)
Algunos aparatos de la casa, p. 266	Quiz/Listening Activity 5, p. L53 (Side A, track 12)
	Transparencies 48-49
	Workbook Activities 8-9, pp. 124-125
	Quiz/Written Activity 4, p. W72

Notes

Textbook	**Support Materials**

Warm-up: Review *Algunos aparatos de la casa*, p. 266

Para ti: Otros aparatos de la casa, p. 267

Activity 18, p. 267

Oportunidades, p. 267

Activities 19-21, pp. 268-269

Autoevaluación, p. 269

¡La práctica hace al maestro!, Activities A-B, p. 270

A escribir, p. 276

AC/CD: Activity 18 (Side B, track 13)

Quiz/Written Activity 5, p. W73

Video program, Episode 6

Workbook Activity 10, p. 126

Quiz/Listening Activity 6, p. L53 (Side A, track 13)

Notes

Textbook	**Support Materials**
Warm-up: Review *Vocabulario,* p. 271 *A leer,* Activities A-B, pp. 272-275 Review for the test on *Lección 12* Test on *Lección 12*	AC/CD: *La familia hispana* (Side B, track 14) Quiz/Listening Activity 7, p. L54 (Side A, track 14) Quiz/Written Activity 6, p. W74 AC/CD: Activities A-B (Side B, tracks 15-16) Student Test Booklet, Activities 1-12, pp. 103-110 Test Booklet Teacher's Edition, pp. 36-39 Audiocassette/Audio CD listening comprehension test (Side A, tracks 5-8) Oral Proficiency Evaluation Manual, Activities 1-3, pp.38-40 Select an activity from *Capítulo 6* to include in the *Somos así* Portfolio Assessment. Suggestion: Checklist appropriate items on appendices C, D, E, F, G, H, I and J, as needed.

Notes

Capítulo 7, lecciones 13 y 14

Day 1	Textbook	Support Materials
	Warm-up: Review expressions of doubt and emotion	AC/CD: *Las noticias* (Side A, track 1)
	Review the test on *Lección 12*	AC/CD: Activity 1 (Side A, track 2)
	Chapter preview: Discuss chapter opener, pp. 278-279	Quiz/Listening Activity 1, p. L55 (Side B, track 15)
	Las noticias, p. 280	Transparency 50
	Activity 1, p. 280	AC/CD: *El Uruguay* (Side A, track 3)
	Conexión cultural, p. 281	Quiz/Listening Activity 2, p. L55 (Side B, track 16)
	Activity 2, p. 282	Workbook Activity 1, p. 127
	Las noticias (continuación), p. 282	AC/CD: *Las noticias (continuación)* (Side A, track 4)
	Activity 3, p. 283	AC/CD: Activities 3-4 (Side A, tracks 5-6)
	Algo más, p. 283	Quiz/Listening Activity 3, p. L56 (Side B, track 17)
	Activity 4, p. 283	Workbook Activity 2, p. 128
	Para ti: Más sobre las noticias, p. 283	Quiz/Written Activity 1, p. W75
	Oportunidades, p. 284	Quiz/Listening Activity 4, p. L56 (Side B, track 18)
	Activities 5-6, pp. 284-285	Workbook Activities 3-5, pp. 129-131
	Idioma, p. 285	Quizzes/Written Activities 2-3, p. W76
	Activity 7, p. 286	

Notes

Textbook	**Support Materials**
Warm-up: Review *El pretérito perfecto y el participio*, p. 285	AC/CD: Activities 10-11 (Side A, tracks 7-8)
Activities 8-10, pp. 286-287	Quiz/Listening Activity 5, p. L56 (Side B, track 19)
Para ti: Proverbios y dichos, p. 287	Workbook Activities 6-7, pp. 132-133
Activity 11, p. 288	Quiz/Written Activity 4, p. W77
Algo más, p. 288	AC/CD: *En la televisión* (Side B, track 9)
Activities 12-15, pp. 289-290	Quiz/Written Activity 5, pp. W78-W79
En la televisión, pp. 290-291	AC/CD: Activities 16-17 (Side B, tracks 10-11)
Activities 16-17, p. 291	Workbook Activity 8, p. 134
Algo más, p. 291	Quiz/Written Activity 6, pp. W80-W81
Activities 18-20, pp. 292-293	AC/CD: Activity 20 (Side B, track 12)
En la televisión (continuación), p. 293	AC/CD: *En la televisión (continuación)* (Side B, track 13)
Activity 21, p. 294	Quiz/Listening Activity 6, p. L57 (Side B, track 20)
	Workbook Activity 9, p. 135
	AC/CD: Activity 21 (Side B, track 14)

Notes

| **Day 3** | **Textbook** | **Support Materials** |

Warm-up: Review the dialog *En la televisión (continuación)*, p. 293

Activity 22, p. 294

Algo más, p. 295

Activities 23-25, pp. 295-296

Autoevaluación, p. 297

Review *Vocabulario*, p. 299

¡La práctica hace al maestro!, Activities A-B, p. 298

Review for the test on *Lección 13*

AC/CD: Activity 22 (Side B, track 15)

Quiz/Listening Activity 7, p. L58 (Side B, track 21)

Workbook Activity 10, p. 135

Quiz/Written Activity 7, p. W82

Workbook Activity 11, p. 136

Notes

Textbook	Support Materials
Test on *Lección 13*	Student Test Booklet, Activities 1-11, pp. 111-118
En el periódico, p. 300	Test Booklet Teacher's Edition, pp. 39-41
Activity 1, p. 301	Audiocassette/Audio CD listening comprehension test (Side A, tracks 9-12)
Algo más, p. 301	Oral Proficiency Evaluation Manual, Activities 1-3, pp. 41-43
Activities 2-3, p. 301	Select an activity from *Capítulo 7* to include in the *Somos así* Portfolio Assessment. Suggestion: Activity A, p. 298, Appendices B-1 and F-1
Para ti: Más palabras de los periódicos, p. 301	AC/CD: *En el periódico* (Side A, track 1)
	Quiz/Listening Activity 1, p. L59 (Side B, track 22)
	AC/CD: Activities 1-2 (Side A, tracks 2-3)
	Transparency 51
	Workbook Activity 1, p. 137
	Quiz/Written Activity 1, p. W83

Notes

Textbook	Support Materials
Warm-up: Review the dialog *En el periódico,* p. 300	AC/CD: *El Paraguay* (Side A, track 4)
Review the test on *Lección 13*	Quiz/Listening Activity 2, p. L59 (Side B, track 23)
Oportunidades, p. 302	Workbook Activity 2, p. 138
Activities 4-5, p. 302	Quiz/Listening Activity 3, p. L60 (Side B, track 24)
Conexión cultural, p. 303	Workbook Activities 3-4, pp. 139-140
Activity 6, p. 304	Quiz/Written Activity 2, p. W84
Idioma, p. 304	AC/CD: *Las noticias se escuchan por Radio Ñandutí* (Side A track 5)
Activities 7-12, pp. 304-307	Quiz/Listening Activity 4, p. L61 (Side B, track 25)
Las noticias se escuchan por Radio Ñandutí, p. 307	Workbook Activity 5, p. 141
Activities 13-14, p. 308	AC/CD: Activity 13-14 (Side A, tracks 6-7)

Notes

Textbook	Support Materials
Warm-up: Review the dialog *Las noticias se escuchan por Radio Ñandutí,* p. 307	Quiz/Listening Activity 5, p. L62 (Side B, track 26)
Estrategia, p. 308	Workbook Activity 6, p. 142
Activity 15, p. 309	Quiz/Written Activity 3, p. W85
Repaso rápido, p. 309	AC/CD: Activities 15-16 (Side A, tracks 8-9)
Activity 16, p. 309	Quiz/Written Activity 4, p. W86
Idioma, p. 310	AC/CD: Activity 17 (Side B, track 10)
Activities 17-20, pp. 310-312	Quiz/Listening Activity 6, p. L63 (Side B, track 27)
El fútbol, p. 312	Workbook Activities 7-8, pp. 143-144
Algo más, p. 313	Quiz/Written Activity 5, p. W87
Activities 21-22, p. 313	AC/CD: Activity 20 (Side B, track 11)
	AC/CD: *El fútbol* (Side B, track 12)
	Transparencies 52-53
	AC/CD: Activity 21 (Side B, track 13)
	Workbook Activity 9, p. 145
	Quiz/Written Activity 6, p. W88

Notes

Day 7	Textbook	Support Materials
	Warm-up: Review *El fútbol,* pp. 312-313	Workbook Activity 10, p. 146
	Autoevaluación, p. 313	Quiz/Listening Activity 7, p. L64 (Side B, track 28)
	¡La práctica hace al maestro! Activities A-B, p. 314	Quiz/Written Activity 7, p. W89
	A leer, Activities A-B, pp. 316-319	AC/CD: *Ayuda para las víctimas del terremoto* (Side B, track 14)
		AC/CD: Activities A-B (Side B, tracks 15-16)

Notes

Textbook	Support Materials

Warm-up: *Repaso,* p. 321
A escribir, p. 320
Review for the test on *Lección 14*
Test on *Lección 14*
	Video Program, Episode 7
	Student Test Booklet, Activities 1-12,
	   pp. 119-126
	Test booklet Teacher's Edition, pp. 41-44
	Audiocassette/Audio CD listening
	   comprehension test (Side A, tracks 13-16)
	Oral Proficiency Evaluation Manual,
	   Activities 1-3, pp. 44-46
	Select an activity from *Capítulo 7* to include
	   in the *Somos así* Portfolio Assessment.
	   Suggestion: Checklist appropriate items
	   on appendices C, D, E, F, G, H, I and J,
	   as needed.

Notes

Capítulo 8, lecciones 15 y 16

Day 1	Textbook	Support Materials
	Warm-up: Review *La voz pasiva*, p. 310	AC/CD: *Las próximas vacaciones* (Side A, track 1)
	Review the test on *Lección 14*	Quiz/Listening Activity 1, p. L65 (Side A, track 1)
	Chapter preview: Discuss the chapter opener, pp. 322-323	Transparency 54
	Las próximas vacaciones, p. 324	AC/CD: Activity 1 (Side A, track 2)
	Activity 1, p. 325	AC/CD: *La tortilla española* (Side A, track 3)
	Para ti: La corrida de toros, p. 325	Quiz/Listening Activity 2, p. L65 (Side B, track 2)
	Conexión cultural, p. 325	Workbook Activity 1, p. 147
	Activity 2, p. 326	AC/CD: *Las próximas vacaciones (continuación)* (Side A, tracks 4-5)
	Las próximas vacaciones (continuación), p. 326	Workbook Activity 2, p. 148
	Activities 3-4, p. 327	Quiz/Written Activity 1, p. W91
	Repaso rápido, p. 327	AC/CD: Activities 3-5 (Side A, tracks 6-8)
	Activities 5-6, pp. 327-328	Quiz/Written Activity 2, p. W92
	Idioma, p. 328	Quiz/Listening Activity 3, p. L66 (Side A, track 3)
	Activities 7-11, pp. 329-330	Workbook Activities 3-5, pp. 149-151
		Quizzes/Written Activities 3-4, pp. W93-W94
		AC/CD: Activities 7, 9 and 10 (Side A, tracks 9-11)

Notes

Textbook	Support Materials
Warm-up: Have students tell what they will do next weekend	AC/CD: Activity 12 (Side B, track 12)
Algo más, p. 331	Quiz/Listening Activity 4, p. L66 (Side A, track 4)
Activities 12-14, pp. 331-332	Workbook Activity 6, p. 152
Las reservaciones, p. 333	AC/CD: Activity 13 (Side B, track 13)
Activities 15-16, p. 334	AC/CD: *Las reservaciones* (Side B, tracks 14-15)
Para ti: Otra palabras y expresiones, p. 334	Quiz/Listening Activity 5, p. L67 (Side A, track 5)
Algo más, p. 335	Workbook Activity 7, p. 153
Activities 17-18, p. 335	AC/CD: Activities 15-16 (Side B, tracks 16-17)
Idioma, p. 336	Workbook Activity 8, p. 154
Activities 19-22, pp. 337-338	Quiz/Written Activity 5, p. W95
	Quiz/Listening Activity 6, p. L67 (Side A, track 6)
	Workbook Activities 9-10, pp. 155-156
	Quizzes/Written Activities 6-7, pp. W95-W96
	AC/CD: Activity 20 (Side B, track 18)

Notes

Textbook	Support Materials
Warm-up: Review *El futuro de los verbos irregulares,* p. 336	Quiz/Listening Activity 7, p. L68 (Side A, track 7)
Oportunidades, p. 339	Workbook Activity 11, p. 157
Activity 23, p. 339	AC/CD: Activity 25 (Side B, track 19)
En la agencia de viajes, p. 340	Workbook Activity 12, p. 158
Activities 24-26, pp. 340-341	
Autoevaluación, p. 341	
¡La práctica hace al maestro!, Activities A-B, p. 342	
Review for the test on *Lección 15*	

Notes

Textbook	Support Materials

Test on *Lección 15*
En el mostrador de la aerolínea, p. 344
Activities 1-2, pp. 344-345
Algo más, p. 345
Activity 3, p. 345

Student Test Booklet, Activities 1-13,
  pp. 127-134
Test Booklet Teacher's Edition, pp. 44-46
Audiocassette/Audio CD listening
  comprehension test (Side B, tracks 17-20)
Oral Proficiency Evaluation Manual,
  Activities 1-3, pp. 47-49
Select an activity from *Capítulo 8* to include
  in the *Somos así* Portfolio Assessment.
  Suggestion: Activity 11, p. 330,
  Appendices B-1 and F-1
AC/CD: *En el mostrador de la aerolínea*
  (Side A, tracks 1-2)
Quiz/Listening Activity 1, p. L69 (Side A,
  track 8)
Transparency 55
Workbook Activity 1, p. 159
AC/CD: Activities 1-2 (Side A, tracks 3-4)
Quiz/Listening Activity 2, p. L70 (Side A,
  track 9)
Transparency 56
Quiz/Written Activity 1, pp. W97-W98

Notes

Textbook	Support Materials
Warm-up: Review the dialog *En el mostrador de la aerolínea*, p. 344	AC/CD: *España* (Side A, track 5)
Review the test on *Lección 15*	Quiz/Listening Activity 3, p. L71 (Side A, track 10)
Activity 4, p. 346	Workbook Activity 2, p. 160
Oportunidades, p. 346	Quiz/Listening Activity 4, p. L71 (Side A, track 11)
Conexión cultural, p. 347	AC/CD: Activities 7-8 (Side A, tracks 6-7)
Activity 5, p. 348	AC/CD: *Bienvenidos a su vuelo número 108* (Side A, track 8)
Idioma, p. 348	Quiz/Listening Activity 5, p. L72 (Side A, track 12)
Activities 6-9, pp. 349-350	Workbook Activities 5-7, pp. 163-165
Para ti: Proverbios y dichos, p. 350	Quiz/Written Activity 4, pp. W100-W101
Activity 10, p. 351	AC/CD: Activity 12 (Side A, track 9)
Bienvenidos a su vuelo número 108, p. 351	
Activity 11, p. 352	
Algo más, p. 352	
Activities 12-13, p. 353	

Notes

Warm-up: Review *El condicional de los verbos irregulares*, p. 352

Activity 14, p. 354

En taxi al hotel, p. 354

Activities 15-16, pp. 354-355

Para ti: ¿A qué hora?, p. 355

En la recepción del hotel, p. 355

Activity 11, p. 356

Algo más, p. 356

Activity 18, p. 356

Oportunidades, p. 357

Activity 19, p. 357

Conexión cultural, p. 358

Activities 20-21, p. 359

Algo más, p. 360

Activities 22-23, pp. 360-361

AC/CD: *En taxi al hotel* (Side A, track 10)

AC/CD): Activities 15-16 (Side A, tracks 11-12)

AC/CD): *En la recepción del hotel* (Side A, tracks 13-14)

Quiz/Listening Activity 6, p. L73 (Side A, track 13)

Workbook Activity 8, p. 166

AC/CD: Activities 17-18 (Side A, tracks 15-16)

Quiz/Written Activity 5, p. W102

Workbook Activity 9, p. 167

Quiz/Written Activity 6, p. W103

AC/CD: Activities 22-23 (Side B, tracks 17-18)

Notes

Textbook	Support Materials
Warm-up: Review *El condicional de probabilidad*, p. 360 *Autoevaluación*, p. 361 *¡La práctica hace al maestro!* Activities A-B, p. 362 *A leer:* Acts A-B, pp. 364-369	Workbook Activity 10, p. 168 Quiz/Listening Activity 7, p. L74 (Side A, track 14) AC/CD: *Lázaro cuenta su vida y de quien fue hijo* (Side B, track 19) AC/CD: Activities A-B (Side B, tracks 20-21) Quiz/Written Activity 7, p. W104

Notes

Textbook	Support Materials

Warm-up: Review *Repaso*, p. 371
A escribir, p. 370
Review for the test on *Lección 16*
Test on *Lección 16*
	Video Program, Episode 8
	Student Test Booklet, Activities 1-12,
	    pp. 135-142
	Test Booklet Teacher's Edition, pp. 47-49
	Audiocassette/Audio CD listening
	    comprehension test (Side B, tracks 21-24)
	Oral Proficiency Evaluation Manual,
	    Activities 1-3, pp. 50-52
	Select an activity from *Capítulo 8* to include
	    in the *Somos así* Portfolio Assessment.
	    Suggestion: Checklist appropriate items
	    on appendices C, D, E, F, G, H, I and J,
	    as needed.

Notes

Capítulo 9, lecciones 17 y 18

Textbook	Support Materials
Warm-up: Review *El condicional de probabilidad,* p. 360	AC/CD: *Asistir a la universidad* (Side A, tracks 1-2)
Review the test on *Lección 16*	Quiz/Listening Activity 1, p. L75 (Side B, track 15)
Chapter preview: Discuss chapter opener pp. 372-373	AC/CD: Activities 1-2 (Side A, tracks 3-4)
Asistir a la universidad, p. 374	AC/CD: *Los empleos* (Side A, track 5)
Activities 1-2, p. 375	Transparencies 57-58
Oportunidades, p. 375	Quizzes/Listening Activities 2-3, p. L76 (Side B, tracks 16-17)
Conexión cultural, p. 376	Workbook Activities 1-2, pp. 169-170
Activity 3, p. 377	Quizzes/Written Activities 1-2, pp. W105-W106
Oportunidades, p. 377	AC/CD: Activity 5 (Side B, track 6)
Los empleos, p. 378	
Algo más, p. 378	
Para ti: Más empleos, p. 378	
Activities 4-5, p. 379	

Notes

Warm-up: Review *Más sobre los empleos* and
　Más empleos, p. 378
Activities 6-10, pp. 380-381
Repaso rápido, p. 382
Activity 11-12, pp. 382-383
Idioma, p. 383
Activities 13-18, pp. 384-386
Amigos por correspondencia, p. 387
Activities 19-20, p. 388

Quiz/Listening Activity 4, p. L77 (Side B,
　track 18)
Workbook Activities 3-4, pp. 171-172
Quiz/Written Activity 3, p. W107
AC/CD: Activity 12 (Side B, track 7)
Quiz/Listening Activity 5, p. L77 (Side B,
　track 19)
Workbook Activities 5-6, pp. 173-174
Quizzes/Written Activities 4-5,
　pp. W108-W109
AC/CD: Activity 13 (Side B, track 8)
Quiz/Listening Activity 6, p. L78 (Side B,
　track 20)
Workbook Activity 7, p. 175
AC/CD: Activities 19-20 (Side B,
　tracks 9-10)

Notes

Day 3

Textbook	Support Materials
Warm-up: Review *Amigos por correspondencia*, p. 387	Quiz/Listening Activity 7, p. L78 (Side B, track 21)
Idioma, pp. 388-389	Workbook Activities 8-9, pp. 176-177
Activities 21-25, pp. 389-391	Quizzes/Written Activities 6-7, p. W110
Autoevaluación, p. 391	Workbook Activity 10, p. 178
¡La práctica hace al maestro!, Activities A-B, p. 392	Oral Proficiency Evaluation Manual, Activities 1-3, pp. 53-55
Review for the test on *Lección 17*	Select an activity from *Capítulo 9* to include in the *Somos así* Portfolio Assessment. Suggestion: Activity 18, p. 386, appendices B-1 and F-1

Notes

Test on *Lección 17*
¡Qué suerte tienes!, p. 394
Activities 1-2, p. 395
Estrategia, p. 395

Student Test Booklet, Activities 1-12,
pp. 143-150
Test booklet Teacher's Edition, pp. 49-51
Audiocassette/Audio CD listening
comprehension test (Side A, tracks 1-5)
AC/CD: *¡Qué suerte tienes!* (Side A, track 1)
Quiz/Listening Activity 1, p. L79 (Side B,
track 22)
Transparency 59
Workbook Activity 1, p. 179
AC/CD: Activities 1-2 (Side A, tracks 2-3)

Notes

Day 5	Textbook	Support Materials

Textbook

Warm-up: Review dialog *¡Qué suerte tienes!*, p. 394

Review the test on *Lección 17*

Para ti: Proverbios y dichos, p. 396

El lenguaje del cuerpo, p. 396

Activity 3, p. 396

Repaso rápido, p. 397

Activities 4-5, p. 397-398

Idioma, pp. 398-399

Activities 6-10, pp. 399-401

Support Materials

Quiz/Listening Activity 2, p. L79 (Side B, track 23)

Transparency 60

Workbook Activity 2, p. 180

Quiz/Listening Activity 3, p. L80 (Side B, track 24)

Workbook Activities 3-4, pp. 181-182

Quiz/Written Activity 1, p. W111

Quiz/Listening Activity 4, p. L80 (Side B, track 25)

Workbook Activities 5-7, pp. 183-186

Quizzes/Written Activities 2-3, p. W112-W113

AC/CD: Activity 8 (Side A, track 4)

Notes

Textbook	**Support Materials**
Warm-up: Review the geographical location of Spanish-speaking countries.	Quiz/Listening Activity 5, p. L81 (Side B, track 26)
Conexión cultural, pp. 402-403	Transparencies 61-62
Algo más, p. 404	Workbook Activities 8-9, pp. 187-189
Para ti: Más países del mundo, p. 404	Quiz/Listening Activity 6, p. L82 (Side B, track 27)
Activities 11-17, pp. 405-407	Quizzes/Written Activities 4-5, pp. W114-W116
Autoevaluación, p. 407	AC/CD: Activities 12 and 16 (Side A, tracks 5-6)

Notes

Textbook	Support Materials
Warm-up: Practice *Vocabulario,* p. 409	Workbook Activity 10, p. 190
¡La práctica hace al maestro!, Activities A-B, p. 408	Quiz/Written Activity 6, p. W117
A leer, Activities A-B, pp. 410-417	Oral Proficiency Evaluation Manual, Activities 1-3, pp. 56-58
	AC/CD: *Lázaro cuenta su vida y de quien fue hijo (continuación)* (Side B, track 7)
	AC/CD: Activities A-B (Side B, tracks 8-9)
	Quiz/Listening Activity 7, p. L82 (Side B, track 28)
	Quiz/Written Activity 7, p. W118

Notes

Textbook	**Support Materials**
Warm-up: Review *Repaso,* p. 419	Video Program, Episode 9
A escribir, p. 418	Student Test Booklet, Activities 1-12,
Review for the test on *Lección 18*	pp. 151-158
Test on *Lección 18*	Test Booklet Teacher's Edition, pp. 52-54
	Audiocassette/Audio CD listening
	comprehension test (Side A, tracks 6-10)
	Select an activity from *Capítulo 9* to include
	in the *Somos así* Portfolio Assessment.
	Suggestion: Checklist appropriate items
	on appendices C, D, E, F, G, H, I and J,
	as needed.

Notes

Capítulo 10, lecciones 19 y 20

Day 1	Textbook	Support Materials
	Warm-up: Review *El subjuntivo: un resumen,* p. 398-399	AC/CD: *Un amigo por e-mail* (Side A, track 1)
	Review the test on *Lección 18*	Quiz/Listening Activity 1, pp. L83-L84 (Side B, track 29)
	Chapter preview: Discuss the chapter opener, pp. 420-421	Transparency 63
	Un amigo por e-mail, p. 422	Workbook Activity 1, p. 191
	Activities 1-3, pp. 422-423	AC/CD: Activities 1-2 (Side A, tracks 2-3)
	Conexión cultural, p. 423	Quiz/Listening Activity 2, p. L85 (Side B, track 30)
	Activities 4-5, p. 424	
	Oportunidades, p. 424	Workbook Activity 2, p. 192
	Activity 6, p. 425	Quiz/Written Activity 1, p. W119
	Repaso rápido, p. 425	Workbook Activities 3-5, pp. 193-194
	Para ti: Proverbios y dichos, p. 426	Quiz/Written Activity 2, p. W120
	Activities 7-10, pp. 426-427	AC/CD: Activity 7 (Side A, track 4)
	Estrategia, p. 427	Quiz/Listening Activity 3, p. L86 (Side B, track 31)
	Activities 11-12, pp. 428-429	
	Autoevaluación, p. 429	Workbook Activities 6-8, pp. 195-196
	¡La práctica hace al maestro!, Activities A-B, p. 430	Quizzes/Written Activities 3-4, pp. W121-W122
	Review for the test on *Lección 19*	

Notes

Test on *Lección 19*
Un nuevo mundo, p. 432
Activities 1-2, p. 433
Para ti: Quisiera, p. 433
Conexión cultural, p. 433

Student Test Booklet, Activities 1-11,
  pp. 159-164
Test Booklet Teacher's Edition, pp. 54-56
Audiocassette/Audio CD listening
  comprehension test (Side A, tracks 11-14)
Oral Proficiency Evaluation Manual,
  Activities 1-3, pp.59-61
Select an activity from *Capítulo 10* to
  include in the *Somos así* Portfolio
  Assessment.
  Suggestion: Activity 12, p. 428,
  Appendices B-1 and F-1
AC/CD: *Un nuevo mundo* (Side B, track 5)
Quiz/Listening Activity 1, p. L87 (Side B,
  track 33)
Transparency 64
Workbook Activity 1, p. 197
AC/CD: Activities 1-2 (Side B, tracks 6-7)
Quiz/Listening Activity 2, p. L87 (Side B,
  track 33)
Workbook Activity 2, p. 198
Quiz/Written Activity 1, p. W123

Notes

Textbook	Support Materials
Warm-up: Review *Un nuevo mundo*, p. 432	Workbook Activities 3-4, pp. 198-199
Review the test on *Lección 19*	Quiz/Written Activity 2, p. W124
Activities 3-5, p. 434	Workbook Activities 5-6, pp. 200-203
Oportunidades, p. 435	Video Program, Episode 10
Activities 6-7, pp. 435-436	Quiz/Listening Activity 3, p. L88 (Side B. track 33)
Oportunidades, p. 436	
Activities 8-11, pp. 437-438	Quiz/Written Activity 3, p. W125
Para ti: ¡Ojo!, p. 438	Workbook, Activity 7, p. 204
Activities 12-13, p. 439	Quizzes/Written Activities 4-5, p.126
Autoevaluación, p. 439	AC/CD: *Oportunidades para el futuro* (Side B, track 8)
¡La práctica hace al maestro!, Activities A-B, p. 440	AC/CD: Activities A-B (Side B, tracks 9-10)
A leer, Activities A-B, pp. 442-445	Student Test Booklet, Activities 1-11, pp. 165-170
A escribir, p. 446	
Review for the test on *Lección 20*	Test Booklet Teacher's Edition, pp. 57-59
Test on *Lección 20*	Audiocassette/Audio CD listening comprehension test (Side A, tracks 15-18)
	Oral Proficiency Evaluation Manual, Activities 1-3, pp. 62-64
	Select an activity from *Capítulo 10* to include in the *Somos así* Portfolio Assessment.
	Suggestion: Checklist appropriate items on appendices C, D, E, F, G, H, I and J, as needed.

Notes

Achievement Test II	Student Test Booklet, Activities 1-24, pp. 171-184
	Test Booklet Teacher's Edition, pp. 59-64
	Audiocassette/Audio CD listening comprehension test (Side B, tracks 19-28)
	Oral Proficiency Evaluation Manual, Activities 1-5, pp. 65-68
	Select an activity from *Capítulos 6-10* to include in the *Somos así* Portfolio Assessment.
	Suggestion: Checklist appropriate items on appendices C, D, E, F, G, H, I and J, as needed.

Notes

Notes

Notes

Notes

Notes

Notes

Notes

Notes

Notes